The Five Commitments of Optimistic Leaders for Children

A Reflective Practice Journal

JUDY JABLON

NICHOLE PARKS

LAURA ENSLER

Printed in the United States of America

First Printing, 2021

Leading for Children
South Orange, NJ 07079

www.leadingforchildren.org

Contents

"A winner is a dreamer who never gives up."

—Nelson Mandela

Welcome

Welcome to *The Five Commitments of Optimistic Leaders for Children: A Reflective Practice Journal*. You may be a parent, teacher, program director, or coach. You may drive the van, create healthy meals for children, manage a large Head Start agency, or own a family child-care home. Because you touch the lives of young children, we invite you to embrace your role as an Optimistic Leader for children, contributing to their success now and in the future. Why do children need us to be Optimistic Leaders? In the words of Marian Wright Edelman, *It's hard to be what you can't see* (Children's Defense Fund, 2018).

How We Got to Optimistic Leadership:
Our Stories

Becoming an Optimistic Leader doesn't happen overnight. We begin by describing how each of us got here and how the ideas in this book evolved from our personal and collective practice.

Judy's Story

I keenly remember how my kindergarten, third-, and seventh-grade teachers made me feel special, and even a little smart. Each had the gift of nurturing relationships and activating curiosity in their students. In junior high school, Mr. Mack was deeply respectful of our opinions about the American literature he loved, and created space for us to express and exchange our ideas in a free-spirited but intellectually rigorous way. They were role models, educational leaders I wanted to follow. They created a sense of equity in the classroom, where all voices mattered. When I began to teach, that's the impact I wanted to have on children. I quickly realized that the more I nurtured respectful relationships with children and the more I was willing to relinquish control so that they had room to express their ideas and investigate what was interesting to them, the more successful the children were and the more satisfied I was as a professional.

Later in my career, when my focus shifted from teaching children to working with the adults in children's lives, I began noticing that the way adults in early learning interact with each other was too often less than stellar. And while we know that children learn best in their relationships with adults, they are also learning by watching how adults model relationships with each other, individually and as part of a group. Shortly after one of the books I coauthored, *Powerful Interactions: How to Connect with Children to Extend Their Learning*, was released I was invited to give a large presentation in Connecticut. At the end of a very dynamic day of professional learning, a director came up to me and said, "I never thought about this until today. If I ever heard one of my teachers talking to children the way I sometimes talk to teachers, I would fire them on the spot. I'm mortified." Of course, I reassured her that she was not alone and that I too was becoming more and more aware of how my tone, my choice of words, or my attitude was often the opposite of what I was asking others to do with children. As I continued to work on *Powerful Interactions*, in too many settings I observed or heard others talk about the challenging relationships and negative program climate caused by gossip, cliques, or lack of communication or commitment. And so much blame. I heard "I can't because of this or that," but rarely did

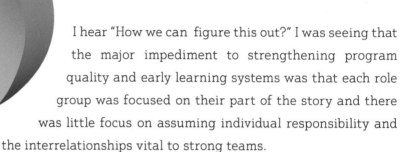

I hear "How we can figure this out?" I was seeing that the major impediment to strengthening program quality and early learning systems was that each role group was focused on their part of the story and there was little focus on assuming individual responsibility and the interrelationships vital to strong teams.

I meet many adults in children's lives who have extraordinary wisdom, lived experience, and so much passion about their work, and yet they are consistently ignored or made to feel *less than*. While we ask educators to find the strengths of children and families and build upon them, professional development in early learning is frequently designed to fix deficits. I described how my teachers in kindergarten, third, and seventh grade helped me to see my power to make things happen — to have a sense of agency. The profound contrast in early learning between how to be with children and the way adults are with each other is striking. Equity among adults is too often absent, while at the same time we ask teachers to pay attention to diversity, equity, and inclusion for children and families.

Changing the narrative in early learning to elevate the wisdom of the adults in children's lives was my impetus for founding Leading for Children. I believe that everyone is a leader for children — and not just a leader, but one who sees a path forward. Seeing people is important — but it's not enough. Becoming leaders for children means practicing self-awareness. It starts with "I have a voice, and now I can strengthen it and use it to its greatest power." This is hard work, and it often means pushing ourselves and others to consider how we are showing up for each other and for children.

I was beginning to assemble the puzzle pieces of Optimistic Leadership from my experiences as a young learner and more than 35 years as an educator in early learning. I firmly believe that every adult in children's lives must embrace the impact they have on how children develop and learn. Moreover, we must own the impact we have on each other and on the emotional spaces where we coexist. We have to be all in and fully committed, because young children need us to be there for them, and not just when it's convenient. Children thrive in a climate of optimism where the adults see a path forward and are willing to persist so that every child succeeds. The framework of Optimistic Leadership was coming together in my mind. My research on leadership confirmed that critical skills include *thinking about impact, cultivating self-awareness, nurturing relationships, refining communication, and activating curiosity.*

In April 2017 I brought together an advisory group of trusted colleagues including Nichole and Laura to introduce the idea of Optimistic Leadership. We sat in a room all day playing with the five key ideas: *impact, self-awareness, relationships, communication,* and *curiosity.* I had been pondering what to call these five ideas — five dimensions, habits, or disciplines. I wanted to emphasize intentionality, as that is key to this practice. Thank you, Khaatim Sherrer El, who suggested "five *commitments.*" Our advisory group loved the idea, especially because too frequently adults in early learning start out committed and then drift to the sidelines because they feel left out of the conversation. By the end of our advisory group meeting, the puzzle pieces had come together as the Five Commitments of Optimistic Leaders. I continued to research and write and began to introduce the work to educators.

In 2018, we were invited to create the first Leading for Children pilot Learning Network in Mississippi, and I knew that Laura and Nichole were the perfect partners to work with me on this. For a year we practiced the Five Commitments of Optimistic Leaders with each other and applied them to every aspect of our thinking as we codesigned the work with our extraordinary partners in Mississippi. Collaborating with Laura and Nichole to create this framework has been one of the most exciting and gratifying experiences of my professional career.

Nichole's Story

I think my path to truly understanding and embracing Optimistic Leadership and the five commitments started when I was a little girl. I grew up in a segregated town in South Carolina, which made me very aware that different levels of respect were given by and to people. This puzzled and saddened me. I would always observe, in order to see how people, especially those in authority, treated others. What I didn't realize at the time was that I wanted to be someone who respected all people and was looking for a role model or guide.

Then in middle school I read a book about the life of George Washington Carver and his rules to live by. One that stuck with me was *Neither look up to the rich nor down on the poor.* It so aligned with my emerging idea of respect for all people that I carried it with me into adulthood.

Fast forward to 2005–2006 when I met Judy. She was facilitating a professional development series and one of the first things I noticed was the way she would greet each person by name and talk with participants during breaks. She made space for each voice. My curiosity was piqued, and I wanted to see if this was genuine respect and if she sustained it over time. Over the following six to nine months, I carefully observed her, and found that it was indeed real and lasting.

I thought, "That's great for Judy, but I am an introvert and I really prefer to sit quietly in my own thoughts rather than talk with people." Yet, I was committed to demonstrating the deep respect I have for all people. I knew I needed something that would get me out of my own head and keep me grounded in that commitment and guide my decisions. That is exactly what the Five Commitments of Optimistic Leaders are to me. For example, when I would rather sneak away to the corner, my commitment to *nurturing relationships* coaxes me out to talk with people. Times when I am quick to make a judgment about a person or a situation, *activating curiosity* guides me into a place of genuine wonder and openness to hearing the perspective of another.

When I think back to how this work with Laura and Judy began, I can clearly see us meeting as a group on Zoom for the first time. Although I knew Judy, it was my first time meeting

Laura. I must admit that I was somewhat intimidated. Judy was someone I'd admired for a long time and I'd done my homework on Laura. She was brilliant! Not only that, I was joining forces with two "northerners" to do this work in the south. How delighted was I when I realized we were all kindred spirits who shared a deep respect for ALL people! Our task was to facilitate a Learning Network (a new way of approaching professional development) that drew out the wisdom of its members to create a shared vision of quality using Optimistic Leadership (a newly developed concept) as one of its frameworks. A piece of cake, right?

The newness and ambiguity of what we were doing required us to be on the same page, reading from the same chapter, in the same tone. Using the Five Commitments of Optimistic Leaders enabled us to do that by:

- Regularly engaging in discussions to *think* about the *impact* we wanted to have on the work we were doing and with each other.

- Committing to *cultivating self-awareness*, which meant sometimes we had to be vulnerable and transparent enough with each other to say, "This is what I'm feeling and here's why."

- *Nurturing relationships*, beginning with each other. We were building this work quickly, which required the ability to be open with and trusting of each other. And we had to realize that *nurturing relationships* with each other wasn't a one and done. To this day, we are still nurturing our relationships, which is what I consider the secret to our effectiveness as facilitators and as a team.

- *Refining communication* with each other, our partners, and our members. This was huge as we as a team learned how to show up with and for each other.

- *Activating curiosity*. What will this work look like? How do we know it's having the impact we desire? What do we do when tensions arise among us?

Looking back, I think that if each of us hadn't been committed to truly embracing the five commitments individually and as a team, we wouldn't have been effective, the amazing story of the Mississippi Leadership for Children Learning Network wouldn't exist, and we wouldn't understand the joy of working together as a team of Optimistic Leaders for children.

Laura's Story

I've been in the early childhood field for over 30 years and have known Judy for most of those years. We have worked closely for a long time and share common beliefs about how the field succeeds and is challenged. Several years ago, after directing several early-childhood programs, I started my early-education consulting firm. As a leader in the field, I found myself disillusioned and craved change to address the inequities I witnessed and the silos our industry had created. I partnered with the Bloomberg administration to plan, develop, and then found FirstStepNYC, a state-of-the-art high-quality early learning demonstration site located in a public elementary school in Brownsville, Brooklyn. In collaboration with FirstStepNYC, we created the first Early Education Leadership Institute for the city, where leaders could come together at the center to work on their own professional development. Judy was essential to centering the program on its mission: to be a place where everyone is seen and heard. Having so much in common, we began to dig deeper into the state of leadership in early education. When Judy shared with me her developing approach of Optimistic Leadership and the attending five commitments, it captured the essence of what FirstStepNYC set out to accomplish and it provided purpose and a pathway to success.

The five commitments are a set of tools that keep all of us on the path, always moving forward with the goal of positive outcomes for all children and families. I knew it was exactly what was needed for those truly invested in serving our most under resourced communities. From the work at FirstStepNYC, it became clear that in order to be effective in our work with children and families, we must support all the adults in the child's eco-system. I wanted to be part of what I knew would be a significant and transformative experience. Several years later, Judy brought the idea to partners in Mississippi and the first Learning Network was born. Building the first Learning Network has been a privilege, particularly working alongside Nichole Parks. Soon after meeting, Nichole and I discovered that we shared many of the same thoughts about the field and what we wanted for children and families. Our Mississippi partners were open, willing, and invested in finding an approach to support early-education leaders that would last. So much training and so many guides, yet very little was having an impact. In nurturing our relationships with each other and with our partners, we had the unique opportunity to define the impact we wanted to have and together construct a plan that took us there.

Having the good fortune to join Leading for Children and become part of the first team to facilitate a Learning Network has been a daunting responsibility for several reasons. First, to do this work with professionalism and accountability required a thorough comprehension and passion for the approach. Second, relationships had to be nurtured with openness, trust, and honesty. For the three of us to become a team, we had to "trust the process" even when it seemed it might be going off the rails. Making it through each of these moments was a victory and a discovery of new and exciting ideas waiting to be cultivated. Third, as facilitators we always want to be models for Optimistic Leadership. Over the three years we have been working together in Mississippi, the three of us have created what we now call our "dance." This has been one of the most satisfying parts of the work and always leads to more learning and greater understanding of Leading for Children's three tenets: *wisdom*, *team*, and *modeling*. Finally, understanding and practicing the five commitments for myself, with each other, and in the network has been astonishing. What we think we know about ourselves as adults is not set in stone; we still have much to learn. Welcoming the wisdom of others is the core of Optimistic Leadership and has become my purpose in this work and in coconstructing the future of early education.

The Reflective Practice Journal is for You

For us, thinking about the Five Commitments of Optimistic Leaders is an ongoing practice. We reflect on our own and in partnership with colleagues. We chose to call it a Reflective Practice Journal with the hope that you, too, will join us in ongoing reflection about how to use the commitments day by day.

What is an Optimistic Leader? As an Optimistic Leader, you're hopeful and willing to find a path forward. You recognize how you affect those around you. Trust us. We know from firsthand experience that optimism and leadership are qualities we can learn and strengthen over time. And by practicing Optimistic Leadership, we model behaviors that help those around us — children and adults — become more confident and effective as well.

Children learn all the time and from everyone who touches their lives. Sometimes what they learn is not what is intended. However, imagine how powerful it would be if children could be surrounded by adults who are intentional decision makers. As Mary Beth Hewitt said, "We need to assume an optimistic view in order for us to feel like we can make a difference in the lives of children. Furthermore, if we want our children to be resilient and optimistic, we need to model it" (Hewitt, 2005).

The journal explores Five Commitments of Optimistic Leaders:

1. *Think impact*
2. *Cultivate self-awareness*
3. *Nurture relationships*
4. *Refine communication*
5. *Activate curiosity*

From our experience as leaders and our extensive research about leadership, the five commitments collectively represent the essential skills of effective leadership. We describe these skills as commitments because intentionality is not something we master — it's something we practice. You'll see that we suggest throughout the journal that you pause and think before you act. To us, that's the first and most important strategy for becoming an Optimistic Leader. We believe that children need adults in their lives who know themselves, who can relate well to others, and who can function effectively within groups. For this reason, we discuss each of the commitments in three ways. First, we invite you to think about you and your identity — who you are and what matters to you. Next, we ask you to explore the commitment by thinking about yourself in relationship with another. And finally, we encourage you to think about the commitment in terms of yourself in a group.

What's Ahead

In Part Two, Optimistic Leadership and the Five Commitments, we introduce the concepts of Optimistic Leadership and the five commitments and explain the three levels of each commitment.

In Part Three, Putting the Five Commitments into Practice, we describe each commitment in detail and illustrate what it means to examine the commitment at each of the three levels: you and your identity, you with another, and you in a group. You'll find stories to illustrate concepts, questions to ignite thinking, and lots of space for reflection.

A Call to Action

We believe that it is imperative for all of us to embrace our role as Optimistic Leaders for children. Each of us and our team at Leading for Children are using the Five Commitments of Optimistic Leadership to guide our practice as early learning professionals on a daily basis. We reference the commitments in our conversations and as we plan experiences with our partners across the country. We make mistakes often, forgetting to *think impact* by starting a meeting without carefully stating the purpose and giving each other time to get on the same page. There are times we neglect to *refine communication* by sending a text or email without noticing how the receiver might experience the tone or misunderstand our meaning. However, together we are also giving ourselves and each other grace when we're clumsy, and are making sure to acknowledge each other's successes.

You might choose to explore the journal on your own, with a thought partner, or as a book study with a group. Focus on the questions that interest you. We invite you to make this part of your daily practice. We truly hope that using this journal on your own and with colleagues becomes a deeply satisfying adventure that allows you to be the leader children deserve.

Thanks for joining us in ensuring that children see Optimistic Leaders every day.

Judy, Nichole, and Laura

Understanding the Five Commitments of Optimistic Leaders

The Why of Optimistic Leaders

We know that young children thrive in an environment of trusting relationships with the adults who care for and educate them. All aspects of children's development are shaped by the relationships they have with the adults in their lives. Imagine an environment of nurturing relationships where every adult in children's lives owns a clear sense of purpose, has a strong voice, and listens and learns from diverse perspectives. These adults are intentional decision makers who collaborate with others to make good things happen. They are optimistic, see a path forward, and have the grit to persevere even when the going gets tough. Consider the possibilities for all children if they could live and learn in an environment with such exemplary models of leadership surrounding them.

Because of systemic racism and inequities, children of color and from underresourced communities do not have the same opportunities as children from more affluent zip codes. To create the next generation of critical thinkers and leaders who will shape an equitable, antiracist society, all children must have confidence in their own sense of agency, a deep belief in their power to make things happen. Children must be surrounded by adults who model that same confidence and can harness their power as Optimistic Leaders to design and implement high-quality early learning programs and healthy communities.

Optimistic Leadership is the foundational principle of the Leading for Children approach to transformative change. Optimistic Leaders commit to an internal effort to change in order to activate external transformation. Systems can grow stronger when the people within them at every level are deeply motivated to think and work in new ways on behalf of a larger vision of quality and exemplary practices for children and families.

Let's take a moment to clearly define what we mean by optimism and leadership. Optimism means hopefulness. It requires confidence about the future and the successful outcome of what we are working toward. Optimists see a path forward and move beyond disappointments to find solutions. Simon Sinek says, "There is a difference between being positive and optimistic. Positivity is telling ourselves and others that everything is good, even if it isn't. Optimism accepts the truth of reality and looks forward to a brighter future" (Sinek, 2020). The Optimistic Leader has conviction that when the inevitable obstacles occur, they can be hurdled with analysis and persistence. Think of optimism as the light at the end of the tunnel, rather than as a smiley face. People with an optimistic outlook have healthier relationships, enjoy better mental and physical health, and live longer. We must embody optimism for ourselves and the children and families we serve, which requires a mindset driven by purpose and focused on outcomes.

Leadership is how you see yourself, your willingness to recognize and own the impact you have on others, and your commitment to take action to effect positive change. Leadership is not defined by a role or title. At Leading for Children, we encourage every adult who contributes to the well-being of young children to recognize their role as leaders. The Optimistic Leader envisions excellence and commits to achieve it.

The Why of the Five Commitments

Optimistic Leaders are committed. A commitment is a pledge, a promise, an undertaking, a responsibility. Commitments take effort and persistence. The Optimistic Leader practices five commitments to be more purposeful and effective, and in turn, to achieve excellence and equity for all children

1 THINK IMPACT

to make informed decisions.

Thinking about impact means that you are intentional about your presence, your words, and your actions and the effect you want to achieve. You decide to pause just long enough to think before you act and to reflect on the benefits and consequences of your actions, both short- and long-term. You can have some control over the outcomes of what you say and do. Whether it is in the moment or planned out in advance, pause and think beforehand so you can shape the result of your action.

2 CULTIVATE SELF-AWARENESS

to guide thought, emotion, and behavior

Practicing this commitment means noticing what's going on with your body, mind, feelings, and behavior. It also means understanding your beliefs and assumptions and how these influence your thoughts and actions. The more you cultivate self-awareness, the more choices you have about how you can show up as a leader.

3 NURTURE RELATIONSHIPS

to support learning and collaboration.

Optimistic Leaders understand the importance of building strong, trusting relationships with children and adults. In all relationships, the more genuine you are, the better the relationship. When you take the time to strengthen connections among children, families, colleagues, and the community, everyone benefits.

4 REFINE COMMUNICATION

for mutual clarity and understanding.

Optimistic Leaders use communication to maintain positive and effective relationships. When you use conversation rather than top-down commands, you can promote purposeful and open conversations that uncover ideas and opportunities and break down barriers. In this way you also create strong teams.

5 ACTIVATE CURIOSITY

to find connections and continue learning.

Optimistic Leaders ask questions, consider possibilities, and make connections with a focus on goals and actions. Using curiosity, you can tackle obstacles, seek opinions from others, and develop new solutions. Rather than worrying about failure, you recognize that mistakes lead to growth and change.

Each commitment is a set of skills you can practice with intention to feel more satisfied and be more effective in your personal and professional life. Practicing each commitment requires you to pause and think so that you can decide how you want to be in that moment. As you use the commitments, notice how they overlap. You often need to use one commitment to help you practice another. For example, imagine that you are about to write an email asking for guidance from your supervisor. You pause to think about how you're feeling about asking for help. Do you feel confident that your questions are reasonable? Are you concerned that your supervisor will think you should be able to figure this out for yourself? Is an email best or should you just pick up the phone and ask? Does your supervisor have so much on her plate that she may react negatively to your questions? As you take time to consider the decision to send the email, you are *thinking impact, cultivating self-awareness, nurturing relationships, refining communication,* and *activating curiosity.* Pausing to be intentional takes a few extra minutes out of your day. However, carefully choosing your words and tone in an email is another step toward a healthier climate among adults and positive change for children.

Three Levels of Each Commitment

To practice each of the five commitments, the first level is about you. We're learning that by tuning in to ourselves —taking time to reflect on who we are and what's important to us—we can increase our effectiveness. The second level is you with another person. As we feel more grounded in ourselves, we can be more intentional about how we interact with others. The third level is you in a group. The impact of our interactions with another person and when we engage with a larger group influences whether those connections will be focused, intentional, and productive. We see these three levels of focus as essential for the practice of the five commitments.

You and Your Identity

This first level of each commitment is about who you are and what matters to you. For many of us who have chosen children's well-being and education as our purpose — to raise and educate children to be the best people they can be—we tend to put ourselves second. At first glance this seems selfless and valiant. But guess what? It leads to exhaustion and burnout and undermines our effectiveness as agents of change and leaders for children. The wisdom of the flight attendant who reminds us to put on our own oxygen mask before assisting others recognizes that we can't be effective in taking care of someone else if we don't first care for ourselves. We want to model this for children every day.

Begin by exploring what matters to you with these questions:

✦ What makes you who you are (your gender, age, race, roles, family, life experience)?

_____
_____
_____
_____
_____
_____

✦ What's important to you at your core (your heart and head, your values, beliefs) and in all the various roles you play (sibling, parent, life partner, educator)?

_____
_____
_____
_____
_____
_____

✦ What and who have been your influencers?

_____
_____
_____
_____
_____

✦ What do you need to feel whole and take care of yourself?

_____
_____
_____
_____
_____
_____

An educator and close colleague shared her responses to the some of the questions about you and your identity. We are deeply appreciative of her willingness to be vulnerable and we promised anonymity.

Our colleague responds: You and Your Identity

What makes you who you are?

My race affects how people see me and how my contributions to the field are underappreciated based on my race. My grandmother had a lot of influence on me. She helped me and provided me with strength. She gave me confidence. I want to show up as a confident woman with a very strong work ethic. I want people to see my commitment to my work, as well as my persistence in accomplishing my goals. Most importantly for me, I want to show this to my daughters and be a role model for them and for other women so that they believe they can achieve things that are in front of them. I want them to be able to conquer the world if they want.

What's important to you at your core and in all the various roles you play?

To me, in all roles, it is important to be reliable and show accountability. It's important to be transparent and gain trust. I value respect, relationships, and work ethics. I want to support others, to be empathic, reliable, and present for them when they need me. I don't separate my role at work or at home or when I'm outside. I'm always the same person. I try to be as transparent as possible in any setting. I don't try to be someone I'm not or try to impress someone.

The late professor of educational psychology, **ASA HILLIARD,** *tells us:* "*Relationships matter more than anything else. Human beings need to be nurtured.*"

You with Another

The second level invites you to think about the commitment with another person: an adult or child, family, friend, or colleague, someone you like or dislike. Relationships are at the core of the work we do in service of young children. For this reason, in addition to the commitment to *nurture relationships*, one of the three levels of each commitment examines how you will practice it as you interact with another person. Here are some questions to guide your reflection about you in relation to another:

✦ What matters to you as you interact with another person?

_____

_____

_____

_____

_____

✦ How do you want to show up with another person?

_____

_____

_____

_____

_____

✦ How do you demonstrate respect for another person?

_____

_____

_____

_____

_____

✦ How do you look for respect from another person?

_____

_____

_____

_____

_____

Our colleague responds: You and Another

What matters to you as you interact with another person?

I want to listen first. It is really important for me to listen attentively, and I try very hard to avoid thinking about what I'm going to say next. Especially in group conversations, I stay quiet because I want to hear it all, take it all in. When I disagree with someone, I try to find the right way and the right time to say so without offending. Rather, I let the person know that I understand their point of view and their opinion. It's important they feel valued and listened to, so we understand the whole picture and we don't make assumptions based on that little piece of information.

How do you want to show up with another person?

I want to show up as present as possible, supportive, and reliable.

How do you demonstrate respect for another person?

I demonstrate respect for the other person by listening attentively, keeping my promises, valuing the other person's ideas and dreams, and supporting her goals.

How do you look for respect from another person?

When I'm looking for respect, I know that I have to respect others first. I cannot ask for something that I'm not giving or willing to give myself. It can be seen in the way you look at the other person, directly into their eyes, or even in a smile. Just be genuine about it, like you really care about it. Sometimes when you have met with the same person several times and they don't even remember your name, you notice that. Or that they'd rather go and talk to the next person. They make you feel like you're invisible.

You in a Group

The third level of practice with each commitment is about how you show up in a group. Group interactions have very different dynamics than one-on-one interactions. To create the strong early learning systems that are vital for all children to thrive, Optimistic Leaders think deeply about this. Too often the adults in the child's ecosystem struggle with collaboration and partnerships. We invite you to think about how you function in a group:

✦ How do you feel in group settings?

_____

_____

_____

_____

_____

✦ How do you want to show up in a group?

_____

_____

_____

_____

_____

✦ How do you ensure that your voice is heard and that you listen to the voices of others without judgment?

_____

_____

_____

_____

_____

✦ What are some ways you contribute to productively influencing a group?

_____

_____

_____

_____

_____

Our colleague responds: You in a Group

How do you feel in group settings?

If it's a new group, I usually feel like I don't belong. It takes some time for me to get comfortable. I start feeling more confident when I get to know each member of that group and I can find commonality. Once I'm comfortable, I can be very loyal to that group. I want to be transparent, and I want them to trust what I'm saying, because I'm not just saying things because I want to, but because I can back them up.

How do you want to show up in a group?

I want to show up as a transparent, loyal, reliable, trusting, and supportive woman.

How do you ensure that your voice is heard and that you listen to the voices of others without judgment?

I want to ensure that I'm being listened to without judgment by providing details and helping others see the big picture. You need to know the details before judging or making assumptions or coming to a conclusion. I want to do that for others as well. I do this by listening attentively and respecting other people's opinions and ideas. I try to avoid taking comments personally and taking their own perspective on topics. I can understand where they're coming from, but it's not about me. I have to think, "Why is it that I'm doing this? What's my real objective?" Because even though sometimes I think that I don't have biases, we all do.

These three levels of focus offer greater depth for practicing the five commitments. Clarifying and acknowledging your identity, then considering yourself in relation to another and within a group gives you more power and helps you to be more accountable. In Part Three, you will learn more about the three levels of each commitment through stories and reflective questions.

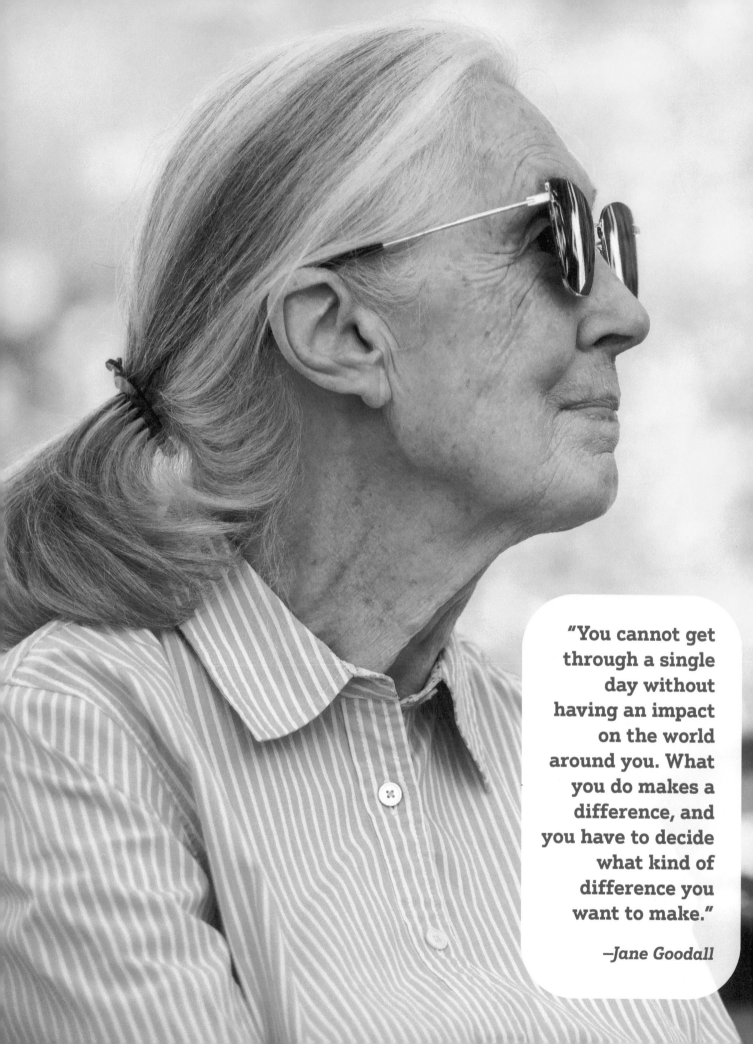

"You cannot get through a single day without having an impact on the world around you. What you do makes a difference, and you have to decide what kind of difference you want to make."

—Jane Goodall

Practicing the Five Commitments

Think Impact

Judy recalls: *It was early in September of my freshman year in college when I submitted my first paper. A week later the professor returned our papers in class. Across the front page of mine, he had written in all caps: THIS READS LIKE THE YELLOW PAGES. DO IT OVER. Humiliated and devastated, I was clueless about how to fix it. When I went to his office to get more feedback, he reiterated that I had to do it again but offered no specific suggestions. The professor's comment squashed my confidence as a first-year college student and negatively affected the entire semester. All these years later I still wonder what impact he intended. Was he aware of the effect his comments would have on me? Was his goal to help me improve my writing, or was it to make me feel a certain way? Did he stop and think about what he was doing or was he just trying to get through his students' papers quickly because he was busy?*

***Think impact* to make informed decisions** means anticipating outcomes. Everything you do and say has an outcome. Ideally, it's an optimistic and desirable result. On the other hand, the impact of your actions has unintended consequences. This was the case in Judy's story. The direction it goes depends on intention and attention. The Optimistic Leader has intention and makes decisions guided by purpose. Whether in your personal or professional life, you can control the impact you have.

Consider for a moment what it would be like if you considered the results of your actions, in the moment and in the long term. When you take the time to think about what you want to have happen as a result of your decisions, you create results that are important and meaningful for you and those around you. In your personal and professional life, thoughtful decisions lead to better outcomes. Most of us have experienced leaders who neglected to think about how decisions would unfold and ended up on the receiving end of bad choices.

Rather than simply addressing events in this moment, take enough time to reflect on how your actions will unfold over time. When you think impact, your decisions are more likely to have the intended effect on children, families, and colleagues. Practicing this commitment means giving yourself time and space to decide how you want to adjust your actions and words to create your intended outcome. Whether entering your classroom in the morning, having a parent conference, leading a meeting, or sending an email, take a moment to ask yourself, "What do I want to have happen?" Contemplating how your decisions will evolve over time allows you to act with intention rather than in reaction.

Let's consider an everyday scenario and then look at how the outcome could be different if we practice *think impact*. Sophia is on autopilot as her very long day winds down.

> *Arriving home cranky from an exhausting day at work, Sophia can feel fatigue in her bones and wants nothing more than a relaxing evening to replenish her energy. Her irritability increases when she sees the morning's dirty dishes in the sink, the dog barking to go outside, and her daughter, Nahid, on the phone in the next room. She snaps at Nahid, "Hang up and take out the dog." As Nahid heads out the door, Sophia adds, "You were supposed to clean up the kitchen." Returning from a quick dog walk, Nahid does the dishes in silence, goes to her room, and shuts the door. They do not speak for the remainder of the evening.*

Sophia knows what she needs but neglects to consider how her words and actions will impact Nahid and their evening.

Notice how she can shape an entirely different experience by pausing to reflect on the evening she wants. She can choose to create a positive climate at home, enjoy the outdoors, and spend quality time with her daughter.

> *Arriving home cranky from an exhausting day at work, Sophia can feel fatigue in her bones and wants nothing more than a relaxing evening to replenish her energy. As she pulls into the parking lot of her building, she turns off the car, then rests her head on the steering wheel to close her eyes and take a breath. She envisions the evening that will help her refuel. After one more deep breath, she walks to her*

apartment. Opening the door, she sees the dishes in the sink and hears the dog barking. Feeling her body immediately tense up, she says to herself, "Settle down." She decides to go straight to her bedroom to wash her face and change her clothes. She writes a quick note to her daughter that says: "Hi–I hope you had a good day. Join me for a walk with the dog? Can you finish up your call in a few minutes?" Minutes later, Nahid hangs up and together they take a walk, exchanging stories from their day. Thirty minutes later, Sophia asks Nahid to do the dishes while she begins cooking dinner. Relaxed and connected, they work side by side, continuing their conversation.

In this scenario, Sophia's brief pause before getting out of the car to reset by thinking about what she needs and quieting her mental static allows her to shape an experience that has a positive impact on her and her daughter. A good evening leads to a better night of sleep. Being more rested in the morning means that Sophia can show up more effectively at work the next day. The ripples of *thinking impact* are significant.

In Part Two we introduced the three levels of the commitments—you and your identity, you in relationship with another, and you in a group—and encouraged you to do some big-picture reflections. On the next page, we invite you to reflect on what matters to you for each level of the commitment to *think impact*.

Think Impact: You and Your Identity

This first level of the commitment to *think impact* is about you and what matters to you.

❖ As you reflect on who you are and what really matters to you—your why—what is the impact you want to have on the world?

_____

_____

_____

_____

_____

_____

_____

❖ What has shaped the impact you want to have on the world (gender, race, age, roles, family, life lessons and experiences both personal and professional, individuals who have touched your life)?

_____

_____

_____

_____

_____

_____

_____

_____

❖ Think about specific ways you want to have an impact day by day.

_____

_____

_____

_____

_____

_____

_____

_____

❖ In what ways do you notice how your impact shifts in the various roles you have, personally and professionally?

_____

_____

_____

_____

_____

_____

_____

❖ Think about areas of your life where you may be having impact. How do you find out if that is true?

_____

_____

_____

_____

_____

Let's look at an example of *think impact: you and your identity.*

Meet Raashad, a Head Start teacher working with three- and four-year-olds in Chicago. When Raashad reflects on **think impact: you and your identity**, he understands that so many of his attitudes and beliefs about teaching began when he was a little boy. His dad was a truck driver and away for long periods of time. When his dad came home, he would bring Raashad to school. Raashad remembers how his preschool teacher made a point of connecting with his dad. This was very important to him as a little boy and strengthened his relationship with his father. This early experience informs his commitment to be sure that when his students begin the school year, he makes a concerted effort to get to know each child's family. He wants to be sure that the families in class understand that forging strong, positive partnerships with teachers serves their children well. He believes that when children see the important adults in their lives having strong positive relationships with each other, they feel safe and nurtured. With this impact as a guidepost, he makes intentional decisions when the new school year begins. He wants children and families to have a positive experience right from the start. He sends by mail two notes before the opening of school:

- A note to children letting them know how excited he is to meet them and their families, including a picture of himself with his family

- A note to families introducing himself, welcoming them to their child's new classroom, including some basic information to prepare them for the year

Think Impact: You with Another

The second level of the commitment to *think impact* comes into play as you interact with one other person.

❖ When you interact with one other person, what's the impact you want to have?

_____

_____

_____

_____

_____

❖ What factors contribute to the impact you want to have on your interactions with one other person?

_____

_____

_____

_____

_____

❖ In what ways does your impact on another person shift depending on the person or the situation?

_____

_____

_____

_____

_____

❖ In what ways does the impact you want to have get derailed by the reaction of another person?

_____

_____

_____

_____

_____

To illustrate *think impact: you with another*, let's continue with Raashad's story.

> *As Raashad thinks about his first interactions with each new family, he reflects on the commitment* **think impact: you with another**. *He wants to be sure to convey his belief in open, honest, trusting, and two-way partnerships. He thinks about how he will convey his respect for each family as their child's first teacher. He wants them to know that he is listening to them and that their voices matter most in their child's learning. He wants to be sure he offers them choices about how they can participate in their child's learning and in classroom experiences. In addition to the introductory letters he mails to children's homes, he sends an email to every family, offering them the choice of a home visit, a classroom visit, or both, prior to the opening of school. He recognizes that every family is different and has different levels of comfort around having outsiders come into their homes.*

Think Impact: You in a Group

The third level of the commitment is about how you show up in a group.

❖ What influences whether or not you want to have an impact on the group?

_____

_____

_____

_____

_____

_____

❖ Are there particular groups in which you care more about your impact? Why?

_____

_____

_____

_____

_____

_____

❖ Do you take responsibility for the impact you have on the group?

_____

_____

_____

_____

_____

❖ How do you know whether you are having an impact on a group? Think about how your impact might be effective or undermining for the group.

_____

_____

_____

_____

_____

Let's continue with Raashad's story about *think impact: you in a group.*

Raashad applies **think impact: you in a group** *during the first staff meeting of the school year. Sitting at a table with his close colleagues, he begins to get uncomfortable when Pamela, the director, starts talking about home visits. Raashad's discomfort increases as a collective groan moves through the room. He thinks, "This happens all the time, but today I'm going to address it." Before he speaks up, Pamela, with a slightly irritated tone in her voice, says, "I know a lot of you feel burdened by home visits. How many of you have them scheduled?" Raashad looks around the room and sees his colleagues' unease. This same conversation happens every new school year without a resolution. He decides that he's ready to take action. Checking to make sure his tone is open-minded and not annoyed, he asks, "Before we move on with scheduling, could we take a few moments to notice how everyone is feeling about home visits and to* *be curious about why the visits feel so hard? I'd like to share a personal story. I remember when I was in preschool, my dad was often on the road driving a truck. But when he was home, he brought me to school. My preschool teacher made a point of getting to know his name, and talked with him in the morning, and it really changed how I saw my dad. I know that home visits take extra time. But they are really important, and for many children it is a way for them to know we care about their parents." Martha looks at Raashad and says, "Thanks for being vulnerable. Your story does put some perspective on home visits for me." Others begin to nod in agreement and the tension in the room seems to fade. Raashad speaks up again. "We know that it takes a week to do the visits. Let's support each other and come back with success stories." Pamela acknowledges Raashad for raising the issue and thanks him for telling his personal story. Others talk about why home visits can be hard and share discomfort and insecurities about entering someone's home. Raashad's intentional decisions produced a positive change for everyone.*

When we *think impact*, we own that our words and actions have the power to humiliate, motivate, hurt, heal, frighten, or comfort. As Optimistic Leaders, we invite you to practice the commitment to *think impact* so that children can learn and grow in safe, comfortable environments and have adults around them who model intentionality.

Thinking About Your Practice

1. Think about what it would be like if you and those around you thought more about the impact of your words and actions. How might the relationships and interactions in your setting change? How might the emotional climate of your workplace improve?

_____

_____

_____

_____

_____

_____

2. As you practice *think impact*, consider these questions:

❖ Why is it important to think about the impact of your decisions?

_____
_____
_____
_____
_____
_____
_____
_____
_____

❖ In what ways are you already effective in thinking about the impact of your decisions?

_____
_____
_____
_____
_____
_____
_____
_____

❖ How can you use your past decisions to better equip you to make future decisions?

_____
_____
_____
_____
_____
_____
_____

❖ How will you stay focused on the impact of your actions?

_____

_____

_____

_____

_____

_____

_____

_____

3. Collect a few examples of how you begin to practice this commitment at each of the three levels.

_____

_____

_____

_____

_____

_____

_____

_____

_____

"It was when I realized I needed to stop trying to be somebody else and be myself, I actually started to own, accept and love what I had."

–Tracee Ellis Ross

Cultivate Self-Awareness

Laura recalls: *One day a colleague asked to have a video call. When the call began, she said she was upset with me about something I had said to her that was "out of character" and disconnected from our relationship. She felt damage had been done and was worried about our professional relationship. She wanted me to apologize. My first reaction was to be defensive. I felt misjudged and thought she knew that I would never intentionally try to hurt her. I sat with this, working hard to imagine what my face was telling her. While I had not yet said a word, she said she didn't think I was really listening to her. I paused and took a deep breath. That pause helped me remember how triggered I get when I feel attacked and that I had choices about how to respond. By paying attention to my own feelings, I was able to activate curiosity, enough that I could ask a few questions. My first question was whether she thought my intent was to hurt her. Thinking for a moment she replied, "No, absolutely not." That let us begin to untangle our feelings about the content of my message and recognize that it was my tone and demeanor that had upset her. We wondered about this together. And as we retraced our steps prior to the difficult moment, we realized we had just left a very intense meeting with no time to debrief and were both on edge. She continued to be curious and asked me how I was feeling at the end of the meeting, to which I replied, "A bit lost and somewhat angry." She said, "Me too." We realized that neither of us had paused with each other, and instead we let our emotions run wild. We acknowledged our gratitude for each other and for the space to be open, honest, and trusting so that we could have a difficult conversation. And I realized that when I get triggered, I tend to react defensively and have a choice to act differently.*

***Cultivate self-awareness* to guide thought, emotion, and behavior** means noticing what's going on inside you and choosing how you want to think, feel, and act. The more you understand yourself, the more you can recognize internal signals that things are off. This allows you to adjust so that you can show up the way you want to. In Laura's story, she made a choice to listen to her colleague rather than stay in a place of annoyance, and through that interaction recognized what upset her and how to navigate her feelings in a more productive way. Self-awareness helps you rely on your strengths and know when you need support to navigate things that may be challenging for you.

Cultivating self-awareness helps with self-regulation — understanding and managing your behavior and reactions. How you handle your feelings affects others around you, whether at home or at work, with other adults and certainly with children. Sigal Barsade describes emotional contagion: when one person's emotions influence the emotions of others (Barsade & O'Neill, 2020).

When you can reframe negative thoughts and feelings and focus on what you can control, you feel more effective and, in turn, more optimistic. When you quiet your fears and harness courage, you are more likely to test out possibilities. Practicing self-awareness means that you are open to challenging your implicit biases, to questioning and considering how others experience you. When you are willing to make mistakes, admit that you don't have all the answers, and most importantly, ask for help, you model what it means to be a clear-headed, open-minded Optimistic Leader.

Here's a scenario with and without the commitment to *cultivate self-awareness*. In the first we meet Paula, a coach, having a difficult day and neglecting to practice self-awareness.

> *Paula, a preschool coach, has had two visits with Julia, a teacher of three-year-olds, early in the year. Julia's goal is to strengthen her interactions with children. Paula wants to support Julia by observing and listening and helping Julia notice when and how she is effective with children. Paula knows that she tends to talk too much during her coaching conversations. Today, Paula arrives in Julia's classroom for an observation a few minutes late after a stressful morning of traffic and phone calls. She greets Julia, spends a few minutes interacting with children, and then observes center time for thirty minutes. Still distracted from the morning's stress, she jots some notes but neglects to take photos that capture Julia in action. When they sit together to discuss the observation, Paula does most of the talking, and then as they begin to wrap up Paula apologizes for talking too much.*

Let's notice how, by practicing the commitment to *cultivate self-awareness*, and helping Julia do the same, Paula can shape a very different and more productive coaching conversation.

> *It's early in the year and Paula, a preschool coach, has had two visits with Julia, a teacher of three-year-olds. Julia's goal is to strengthen her interactions with children. Paula is feeling stressed after a difficult morning of*

traffic and challenging phone calls. She takes a minute to settle herself before entering the classroom. She makes a note to self on her iPad: talk less, listen more. And be sure to take a few photos. As she steps into the classroom, she intentionally relaxes her face to project a calm attitude. "Good morning Julia. So glad to be able to visit today. How's your day going?" Julia replies, "Thanks. We're having a good morning." Paula spends thirty minutes observing, making sure to photograph Julia sitting beside a child and taking care to capture some language Julia uses. Just before they sit together to discuss the observation, Paula reminds herself to listen more and talk less. Paula opens the conversation by saying, "Hi Julia. Give yourself a moment to catch your breath and think about how you're feeling today." Paula stays quiet to notice both how she is feeling in the moment and to give Julia time to think. A few moments pass and Julia, laughing a little, says, "Thanks for that. I'm not sure I've actually let myself breathe today." Paula waits another minute and then continues. "Do you feel ready to look at some photos I took this morning?" "Sure," says Julia. Paula opens her iPad to show a picture of Julia sitting beside a child. Julia says, "I'm not sure what to do when I sit next to them. I want them to explore freely during center time without interrupting their play." Paula replies, "Sitting back and observing their play shows respect and lets you know what they are curious about. Look at this photo of Jacob. Notice what he is doing." Julia responds and they think together about what she might say to let Jacob know that she sees him and is interested in his work. Julia says, "Oh! I guess it's not really interrupting if I talk with them about what they're doing in that moment." The conversation goes back and forth, and by the end, Julia is excited about what she wants to try next.

By using self-awareness to pay attention to how she is feeling, Paula can control her emotions and shape an interaction with Julia that is purposeful and effective. She also models self-awareness by inviting Julia to take a breath and notice how she is feeling.

Now let's look at the three levels of the commitment *cultivate self-awareness: you and your identity, you in relationship with another,* and *you in a group.* We encourage you to engage in the reflection about *cultivate self-awareness* and then look back at what you wrote in Part Two.

Cultivate Self-Awareness: You and Your Identity

The more you know yourself and the choices you make about how you want to show up day to day, personally and professionally, the more effective you can be helping children with social and emotional development. Here are some questions for reflection:

❖ Reflect on who you are and the influences that have shaped you (gender, race, age, roles, family, life lessons and experiences, both personal and professional, and individuals who have touched your life). . .

_____

_____

_____

_____

❖ How would you describe your temperament?

_____

_____

_____

_____

❖ Think about your moods and how they shift and change. When do you feel genuinely relaxed? What gives you joy? What gets you angry? What frustrates you? What motivates you?

_____

_____

_____

_____

❖ How do you navigate new experiences and change?

_____

_____

_____

_____

❖ How do you stay grounded when you feel overwhelmed?

_____
_____
_____
_____
_____

❖ What are some ways you take care of yourself?

_____
_____
_____
_____
_____

Let's look at an example of *cultivate self-awareness: you and your identity.*

As Darlene reflects on **cultivate self-awareness: you and your identity,** she considers her current situation with work and family and tries to understand who she is and how she became this person. Darlene has been the education director at an Early Head Start program for three years. She describes herself as an educator to her core. Prior to this position, she was a lead teacher for more than ten years and is passionate about teaching young children. Married with three children, ages twelve and younger, Darlene comes from a large family that lives nearby. Spending time with her siblings and their families is a priority. She has many friends among her colleagues and is well liked by everyone at her agency. People describe Darlene as a great listener and problem solver. Lately she finds herself answering work emails and texts until 11:00 at night and is completely exhausted. Darlene is beginning to ask herself if perhaps being so helpful to others and taking on their worries as her own is burning her out. She's noticing patterns in her behavior and is thinking about how to set some limits. Her first decision is to turn her phone on "do not disturb" after 7:30 p.m. For the first two weeks she checks her phone anyway but gradually appreciates the limit she's set and is sleeping better.

Cultivate Self-Awareness: You with Another

Relationships and interactions are critical for children's growth and development. When you understand what is important to you about relationships and how you choose to show up, you are a more effective model for children and have a better understanding of how to teach these skills to children. In thinking about self-awareness with another, recognize that each person you interact with is different and brings out different aspects of who you are.

❖ How do you practice self-awareness in your relationships?

_____

_____

_____

_____

_____

❖ What do you need in order to receive feedback from others about how they experience you?

_____

_____

_____

_____

_____

❖ Are there relationships in which you tend to be more self-aware? Why do you think so?

_____

_____

_____

_____

❖ Who makes you uncomfortable and why do you think so?

_____

_____

_____

_____

❖ What do you have to do to keep an open mind in your interactions with others?

_____

_____

_____

_____

_____

❖ How do you use self-awareness to notice and adjust when your style is different from that of another?

_____

_____

_____

_____

_____

To illustrate *you with another* for the commitment *cultivate self-awareness*, let's continue with Darlene's story.

> For Darlene, **cultivate self-awareness: you and another** is about being present and available to the people she cares about. She knows how much she enjoys relationships and being a good friend and thinking partner with family, friends, and colleagues. She is beginning to wonder if she is showing up more for her work colleagues and perhaps falling short with family. When she gets home, usually thirty or forty-five minutes late, she barely has enough energy to be present for her family. She's learning that to have a good evening at home, she has to leave work feeling accomplished, so Darlene sets clear goals for herself each day and she establishes priorities. She works on balancing respect for her colleagues' needs with her own by doing quick self-checks each day that assess her progress on her to-do list. Darlene tries hard not to take on the problems of others but rather to help colleagues solve problems for themselves. To accomplish this, when she finds herself wanting to fix, she visualizes an actual space between herself and the other person.

Cultivate Self-Awareness: You in a Group

Self-regulation is a critical skill for all children to develop. Learning that we can make choices about how to show up in a group empowers us with skills that we can teach children. Knowing how we react in a group — what distracts us, what annoys us, and what makes us shut down — matters. Without this self-awareness, we are more reactive, more resistant, and more emotional. We see this in children as well. When their voices cannot be heard, when they are ignored or when they do not feel equity in the group, they cannot grow and develop this sense of self-awareness that will guide them in their interactions.

❖ How do you feel when you are in a group? Think about how you feel differently depending on the size and makeup of the group.

_____

_____

_____

_____

_____

_____

❖ What are some ways you influence the dynamics of a group?

_____

_____

_____

_____

_____

_____

❖ How do you respond when you perceive a group to have dissonance or conflict?

_____

_____

_____

_____

_____

_____

❖ How do you use self-awareness to notice and adjust how you are showing up to support the dynamics of a group?

_____

_____

_____

_____

_____

_____

Continuing with our example of Darlene, let's notice how she practices *cultivate self-awareness: you in a group.*

> *At the end of a staff retreat, Darlene practices* **cultivate self-awareness: you in a group** *as she reflects on how much she focused on reading the group and worrying about the group's mood rather than simply being a member of the group and engaging in learning with them. On her drive home she thinks about how this pattern is similar to what happens at home. When her family is relaxed and easygoing during dinner, she relaxes. If one of her children is upset or even just quiet, she immediately begins to worry about what might be wrong and what she needs to do to help. This same dynamic happens at work. If members of the team are having a heated discussion about a topic, it makes her anxious and she tries to fix it. This is not how Darlene wants to show up in a group. No one is asking her to be responsible for her family's feelings and no one is asking that at work either. She is working on observing her reactions and sitting with them. As she realizes that too often she senses that something is wrong even when it isn't, she is even more committed to practicing* cultivate self-awareness: you in a group.

To begin practicing this commitment, ask yourself, "Do I pause throughout the day to do a self-check to see how I'm doing right now?" Often the alternative is to suddenly feel so overwhelmed or exhausted that it's like being hit by a brick! *Cultivating self-awareness* is hard work. That's why people shy away from it. We have to be brave, bold, and persistent. We have to keep talking about it and make lots of space to think about it with colleagues.

Thinking About Your Practice

1. Think about what it would be like if you and those around you practiced the commitment to *cultivate self-awareness*. How might the relationships and interactions in your setting change? How might the emotional climate of your workplace improve?

_____

_____

_____

_____

_____

_____

_____

2. Consider these questions.

❖ How does self-awareness guide your thinking, emotions, and behavior? Why is this important?

_____

_____

_____

_____

_____

_____

_____

❖ In what ways are you already effective in using self-awareness to guide your thoughts, emotions, and behavior?

_____

_____

_____

_____

_____

_____

_____

❖ What are some tools you can use to stay present and self-aware while simultaneously considering the perspective of others?

_____

_____

_____

_____

_____

_____

_____

_____

❖ How will you sustain your commitment to self-awareness from moment to moment as you keep colleagues, children, and families in mind?

_____

_____

_____

_____

_____

_____

_____

_____

3. Begin to collect examples of you practicing the commitment to *cultivate self-awareness* at all three levels.

_____

_____

_____

_____

_____

_____

_____

_____

"People will forget what you said, people will forget what you did, but people will never forget how you made them feel."

— Maya Angelou

Nurture Relationships

Nichole recalls: *As a young preschool teacher, I was partnered with a seasoned teacher by the administration. We were close in age and I was excited! I had visions of planning lessons together over coffee and laughs. The reality was different.*

Initially, it was horrible. Our personalities contrasted: She was bubbly while I was quiet and reserved. She was organized and I wasn't. She followed the classroom schedule while I did not. For some time, we either ignored or tolerated each other. Reflecting back, I doubt either of us was aware of how our actions were fragmenting our relationship or negatively modeling relationships for children.

I remember the day we decided to nurture our relationship without ever discussing it. During an art activity that required butcher paper, she'd tear off a piece in a straight line, making the perfect rectangle. I would tear a piece with ragged edges. Finally, she stopped and said, "Just stop tearing the paper crooked!" I replied, "Does it matter? They're just going to get paint on it," as I defiantly tore another crooked page for good measure. There we stood, two adults having a stare-off about butcher paper.

The ridiculousness of it must have shaken us out of our absurd behavior. We each took a deep breath. She tore her next sheet of paper without using the frame (though still a straight edge). And I tore my next piece, careful to use the frame to create a perfectly straight line.

From that day on, we took steps to build a stronger relationship between us. We began with genuinely warm greetings each morning. At nap time, instead of acting as if the other didn't exist, we began having conversations. It wasn't long before we were laughing together and communicating comfortably without saying a word. Instead of irritation and silence, the children were seeing colleagues interacting, laughing, and thinking together.

***Nurture relationships* to support learning and collaboration** means forging positive and productive connections. For both adults and children, learning and growth happen in the context of safe and trusting relationships. As Nichole's story illustrates, relationships don't just happen. All good relationships are open, honest, trusting, and two-way, and they take time and patience to cultivate. In all relationships, the more genuine you are, the better the relationship.

Imagine if all children could experience the mutual respect and trust that comes with strong, positive, trusting relationships. When people feel safe, they are more willing to take risks, ask questions, and make mistakes. As Shinler and Fedor suggest, "In any relationship, it takes positive experiences over time to build trust" (Shinler, 2010, p. 72). It's important to build healthy relationships with the children in your ecosystem and equally important to model for them what healthy relationships between adults look like.

As Optimistic Leaders who nurture relationships, be aware of the difference between personal and professional relationships. Sometimes the relationships that form in professional settings become too personal and, in this case, it is hard to hold on to boundaries. Boundaries can be a hard concept to grasp because we can't see them. The definition of a boundary is the ability to know where you end and where another person begins. Professional boundaries are important because they define the limits and responsibilities of the people with whom you interact in your role. When boundaries are clearly defined, you can be more effective in your role.

Let's look at a scenario between a lead teacher and an assistant teacher at an urban preschool program where, unfortunately, the commitment to *nurture relationships* isn't being practiced. Aubrey, an experienced assistant teacher in her late twenties, has just been placed with LaTanya. LaTanya has an outstanding reputation as a preschool teacher within the school and the community, and Aubrey is excited about the placement.

As Aubrey begins her work with LaTanya in the classroom, she is eager to learn from her and hopes they can talk and plan together. Quickly Aubrey realizes that LaTanya keeps to herself and makes plans independently. Aubrey senses that LaTanya expects her to simply follow along without asking questions or making suggestions. Although Aubrey admires LaTanya's teaching style and appreciates working with her, she feels left out. In her previous positions it was a given that the two teachers planned together. Aubrey feels that she has a lot to contribute to their partnership and so she asks if they can co-plan an activity together. She feels dismissed by LaTanya, who barely acknowledges her. Aubrey struggles with feeling that she is not valued and gradually gets frustrated. Sometimes Aubrey notices herself feeling a bit disengaged during day-to-day routines and learning experiences. She approaches the director about her dilemma and is advised to work it out with LaTanya directly. Aubrey decides to ride out the year with LaTanya and considers requesting a new placement for the following year.

Aubrey is frustrated and unable to contribute productively to the classroom because she is uncertain how to nurture her relationship with LaTanya.

Let's play this same scenario again, and this time, notice how Aubrey practices the commitment to *nurture relationships* and supports LaTanya to do the same.

> As Aubrey begins her work with LaTanya in the classroom, she is eager to learn from her and hopes they can talk and plan together. Quickly Aubrey realizes that LaTanya keeps to herself and makes plans independently. Aubrey feels that she has a lot to learn from talking with LaTanya and can offer ideas that could strengthen the work in the classroom. Aubrey decides to offer feedback to LaTanya about effective teaching moments she notices. One morning Aubrey says, "Yesterday during outdoor time, I was listening to your conversation with children as they used the ramps and balls. It seems like you observe them so carefully and let them know what you see. Each time you did that, the children's faces lit up." LaTanya pauses what she is doing and responds, "Yes. I've noticed that if I call attention to the little actions they take, they repeat them with more intentionality and then begin to attach the language I've modeled to their conversations." Nodding, Aubrey says, "I'm going to try that today when we go outside." LaTanya smiles and replies, "Let me know how it goes." Aubrey feels pretty great because this feels like more back-and-forth conversation than they have had so far. The next day she tries out LaTanya's strategy and after school asks LaTanya if she has a few minutes to hear about her experience. After several days of little chats like this, Aubrey feels more relaxed with LaTanya. Knowing that LaTanya has begun collecting paper towel rolls for some construction activities, Aubrey asks if they might do some co-planning of the learning experiences. Although LaTanya agrees, their conversation is pretty much one-sided as LaTanya describes the lesson plan. Aubrey commits to being patient and accepts that she has made progress nurturing the relationship. They are talking more and LaTanya shared a plan with her before implementing it. Aubrey knows that building a partnership and working as a team with LaTanya will take patience and that she has to prove to LaTanya that she is trustworthy. Little by little things shift and eventually Aubrey asks if she can plan one activity with the children each week. LaTanya reluctantly agrees. As LaTanya sees how Aubrey engages children and is able to promote lot of rich conversation, LaTanya invites

her to plan and lead more experiences. Although the process of forming a partnership is slow, Aubrey recognizes that her patience and persistence is effectively nurturing their relationship.

Sometimes relationships form easily, and everyone can reap the benefits of strong partnerships from the start. Often, however, someone has to do the work of being patient so that trust can grow and mutual respect is allowed to form.

Now let's look at the three levels of the commitment: *nurture relationships: you and your identity, you in relationship with another, and you in a group.* We encourage you to engage in the reflection about *nurturing relationships* and then look back at what you wrote in Part Two.

Nurture Relationships: You and Your Identity

A vital part of early learning is forging strong, positive relationships. The first level of the commitment to *nurture relationships* is about what matters to you. Practicing this commitment offers an opportunity to pause and reflect about your attitudes and values about relationships: what's important to you in relationships and how this varies as you interact with different people. Here are some questions for reflection about *nurture relationships: you and your identity.*

❖ In what ways do you think your identity affects your relationships (race, religion, gender, age, where you were born, and where you live now)?

_____

_____

_____

_____

_____

❖ As you were growing up, what messages did you learn about relationships? In what ways have you used what you learned or had to unlearn it?

Treat everyone with the same respect

Always greet and offer a smile

_____

_____

❖ What are some relationships that have been easy for you in the past? What qualities do they have in common?

_____
_____
_____
_____
_____

❖ What do you find easy about forming relationships? Why?

_____
_____
_____
_____
_____

❖ What's difficult for you in forming relationships? Why?

If I notice that people lack manners and
feel that they are superior.
_____
_____
_____

Let's look at an example of *nurture relationships: you and your identity*.

Angela reflects on **nurture relationships: you and your identity** to gain a deeper understanding of how relationships influence who she is and how she wants to be seen as a leader. Since she was a little girl, she has seen herself as a leader. She was smart in school and a great athlete. People liked her and she liked being with lots of people. When she got her first job in a childcare center, she noticed that not everyone was friendly. The director wasn't a strong leader and reinforced the cliques that formed. Over time and as her positions have changed, she has learned that strong, positive, and nurtured relationships really improve the workplace climate and she actively encourages people to get along. In her current position as administrative assistant to the director *at Great Moments Learning Center, Angela and her supervisor, Fatima, share this commitment to trusting, respectful relationships. The entire team at the center works wells together and shares Angela's values of respect, trust, effective communication, and a strong work ethic. While she likes her position and enjoys working closely with Fatima, when she is offered a position at another program within the same agency, she takes it because there is more responsibility and a higher salary. Shortly after Angela leaves, Fatima also leaves the agency for a new position. Anna, the new director, begins in a few weeks. Angela maintains close relationships with her colleagues at Great Moments and they frequently see each other at agency meetings.*

Nurture Relationships: You with Another

All relationships are by definition with another person. This is a chance to think about how you may shift and change depending on the other person. Many teachers say it is easy for them to form relationships with children but harder to form bonds with the adults at work. Others talk about the challenges they have forming partnerships with families. Anyone who has ever been a classroom teacher knows that some children are easier to connect with than others. Use this reflection to think about individuals — adults and children — and the different types of relationships you have with them.

❖ What type of people do you gravitate toward? Why do you think this is?

_____

_____

_____

_____

_____

_____

❖ Who do you shy away from? Why do you think so?

_____

_____

_____

_____

_____

_____

❖ Do you initiate relationships or wait for the other person to reach out to you? Think about whether this is true or not with different groups — children, colleagues, supervisors, and so on.

_____

_____

_____

_____

❖ What are some ways you can get provoked in relationships?

_____

_____

_____

_____

❖ What factors around power dynamics influence you as you nurture relationships?

_____

_____

_____

_____

Let's continue to explore the example of _nurture relationships: you with another._

For Angela, **nurture relationships: you with another** is about mutual trust and respect. Angela learns from her former colleagues that within two months of Anna becoming director, the atmosphere has changed dramatically. She listens as her peers describe how Anna doesn't listen, gives orders, and challenges people's decisions privately and in front of others. Members of the team are demoralized by her brusque and accusatory style. Some staff members talk about leaving. Angela is disheartened to hear about disrespect at her former workplace. She wonders if this is an opportunity to **nurture relationships** by connecting with Anna in support of her colleagues. At an agency meeting, she sees Anna and musters up the courage to introduce herself. They have a cordial chat. A few days later she sends a short and friendly email to Anna asking if they might have lunch together. Anna agrees.

A very nervous Angela meets Anna at the agency café. Angela asks her how she is enjoying the position and what she is noticing about the team. Anna reports specific ways that team members are productive and supportive of one another. Angela is surprised by Anna's enthusiasm and uses self-control to stay open to learning about Anna. She's somewhat distrustful of things Anna is saying, but at the same time Anna seems genuine. Angela asks, "Anna, do you think members of the team know you are appreciative of their work?" Anna replies, "Why do you ask?" Somewhat disingenuously, Angela replies, "When I was a part of that team, we used team meetings to share successes and it really helped to bolster morale. The work can be stressful and celebrating successes gave us energy." Anna thanks Angela for the suggestion and agrees to try it out. Anna suggests they have lunch sometime later that month. A little proud of herself for taking a brave risk of reaching out to Anna, she agrees to meet.

Nurture Relationships: You in a Group

Individual relationships change when we're in a group. Think about a classroom or a family childcare setting. You may have a strong, positive relationship with individual children, but when they are in a group their behaviors may shift. Perhaps one child gets more reserved. Another gets more easily excitable. The same is true with adults. Picture a staff meeting or workshop. Most often, people sit with the people they already know well or their particular group of friends. It's not uncommon to be able to predict who will speak in a group setting, who will stay quiet, who makes the jokes, who raises the hard questions. Groups have behavioral patterns that become predictable, and when we function on autopilot these patterns can undermine productive thinking and problem solving. Thinking about relationships and groups is a critical part of strengthening early learning systems. Give yourself some time to reflect on the commitment to *nurture relationships: you in a group.*

❖ How do you feel about group settings with children and with adults? Are they comfortable or uncomfortable? Why do you think so?

_____
_____
_____
_____
_____

❖ Reflect on group settings and how you function. What are the benefits and drawbacks of choosing to sit with peers with whom you have a close relationship or choosing to move freely about the group?

_____

_____

_____

_____

❖ When you are in a group setting, do you reach out to meet new people? Describe how you do this.

_____

_____

_____

_____

❖ In a group setting, what are some ways you influence group dynamics productively?

_____

_____

_____

_____

Let's continue to explore the example of _nurture relationships: you in a group._

For Angela, **nurture relationships: you in a group** _means making sure that people are seen and heard. She is pleased to hear from her colleagues at Great Moments Learning Center that they are now spending a few minutes at team meetings talking about successes. One colleague shared that she had seen Anna smile for the first time. Angela is careful not to share with her former colleagues that she has become friendly with Anna. While she is enjoying this new relationship with Anna, her reason for cultivating the relationship is to support the group dynamics of her former team. The situation is unique for Angela and she is interested in how it is unfolding. She is no longer at Great Moments. Anna is not her supervisor and, moreover, Anna's position is more senior than hers. Nonetheless, she realizes that she has power to influence the group because of the trusting relationship she is developing with Anna. As they continue to meet_ *and become more open with each other, Angela begins to ask questions about the team. Angela finds ways to offer feedback to Anna about how she might soften her tone in emails and open meetings by inviting input from the group. At first Anna seems a little defensive, yet she continues to ask Angela for suggestions. Anna gradually describes to Angela how the team is getting stronger and the mood around the office is lighter.*

Nurture relationships matters because every person affects the ability of others to learn with and from each other. The Optimistic Leader builds and models professional relationships that invite others to work toward the goal of learning together. Healthy environments for young children depend on each person's contribution to the dynamics of the group. Whether you are in a classroom with children, a parent meeting, a staff meeting with colleagues in your program, or a national conference with people you hardly know, your interactions with others nurture relationships — both fleeting and lasting — that can support learning and collaboration. As you practice this commitment, as with the other four commitments, you'll notice how they overlap. As you work on *nurturing relationships*, you'll find yourself thinking about *impact, cultivating self-awareness, activating curiosity,* and *refining communication.*

Thinking About Your Practice

1. Think about what it would be like if you and those around you thought more about the commitment to *nurture relationships*. How might the emotional climate of your workplace improve?

_____

_____

_____

_____

2. Here are some questions to think about:

❖ Why is it important to you to nurture and strengthen relationships with your colleagues, children, and families?

_____

_____

_____

_____

❖ In what ways are you already effective at nurturing professional relationships with your colleagues, children, and families?

_____
_____
_____
_____
_____
_____

❖ How do you model trusting relationships for the people around you?

_____
_____
_____
_____
_____
_____

❖ As you reflect on professional relationships that directly impact your work, how are you sustaining ongoing, open dialogue and partnership with each of them?

_____
_____
_____
_____
_____
_____

3. Begin to collect examples of you practicing the commitment — _nurture relationships_ at all three levels.

_____
_____
_____
_____
_____
_____

"Effective leaders are able to say to the person they want to impress most: 'I don't know.'"
—Stacey Abrams

Refine Communication

Judy recalls: *I am from New York. My natural communication style is to speak pretty quickly and use lots of words. When I first began doing workshops for teachers, I copied the presenters I had observed over many years of attending professional development experiences. I had lots of slides with many words on each one and I talked a lot. Of course, I paused periodically to offer the group a chance to think and talk with each other, but mostly I was the one doing the talking.*

Then I had a transformational experience. I was in New Mexico facilitating a workshop for a group of Navajo educators and I naively proceeded with my usual style. I noticed that the group members were quieter than I was accustomed to, and when I asked a question, no one raised a hand but simply talked to each other at their tables. How lucky I was that during the lunch break, one of the teachers, Miss Augusta, offered me feedback. "Your words make us very tired, I just wanted to let you know. And we don't like to be singled out to answer questions. That's not our way." I thanked her and asked what else might be helpful when we returned from lunch. She said, "You talk and then we talk. If you want to know what we're saying, walk around the room but please do not ask individuals to speak out loud. That puts attention on one person and that is not our way." I thanked her and we exchanged a very warm hug. The afternoon was relaxed and the teachers had rich conversations at their tables.

Refine communication **for mutual clarity and understanding** means taking the time to think about the message you want to convey and listening to others to learn about what they think and feel. The definition of *refine* is to remove impurities or unwanted elements and improve something by making small changes in order to be more subtle and accurate. What a great way to think about communicating with intentionality. When you strive to have purposeful, open, back-and-forth conversations, you can uncover opportunities, break down barriers, and create strong teams.

What might it be like if children were surrounded by adults who practiced the commitment to *refine communication*? What if they heard adults using conversation rather than top-down commands to convey messages. Instead of hearing "This won't work," they heard "This is interesting. Let's think together about how we can make this work." Imagine if children were surrounded by conversations of inquiry seeking solutions rather than tirades about roadblocks.

When refining communication, an Optimistic Leader is attuned to the audience and adjusts when necessary without judgment. Communicating may mean less talking and more listening, more open-ended questions, and comfort with silence. It's likely to include pausing before speaking, allowing silences for you and others to collect their thoughts, monitoring your tone, listening well, asking questions, being sensitive to cultural and linguistic diversity, and adjusting your style and delivery to the person with whom you are speaking. To refine communication, think about the impact you want to have on others and practice self-awareness to appreciate diverse perspectives.

Here's a story about a family childcare center owned by Khadija.

> Khadija has two employees, Marta and Kerene, and the three women share responsibilities as a management and teaching team. All three are strong, independent-minded women who have worked together for seven years. While everyone shares responsibility for caring for children and engaging with families, Marta and Kerene share certain overlapping roles that sometimes change without any explicit discussion or clarification. In recent weeks, this lack of clarity has caused extreme tension in the relationships among the three women, especially between Karene and Marta.
>
> Khadija is aware that she has a communication issue with Marta. Every time they meet, she feels like Marta is challenging her. Khadija feels exhausted and exasperated by their interactions and she sees Marta as whiny and annoying. In contrast, Khadija finds Kerene easygoing and reliable and their communication is clear and productive. Khadija finally is fed up trying to work with Marta and wants to enlist Kerene to think about how to get Marta to resign.
>
> Marta is hurt and angry about the way Khadija treats her while favoring Kerene, and is disappointed by Khadija's lack of interest in their mutual investment in creating, developing, and running this family care center.

"'To teach' does not mean 'to talk.' It involves being a good listener and bringing others into productive conversations."

OERTWIG & HOLLAND, 2014

Meanwhile, Kerene is trying to hold her own but becoming more and more frustrated by the way Marta treats her. Marta turns off whenever Kerene needs to talk to her. This dynamic has caused the team multiple disruptions and emotional upheaval, and their families can sense the tension and see that the climate of the program has shifted. Khadija knows she has to make a change yet she cannot tolerate the idea of working it out with Marta. She keeps telling Kerene, "I wish Marta would go."

Let's look at the story of Khadija, Marta, and Kerene apply the commitment to *refine communication*.

Khadija and Marta are not getting along. Neither can figure out what to do and they are stuck. Their miscommunication is affecting Kerene, who relies on both of them for management and operations. Khadija has the self-awareness to understand the impact of their dysfunctional relationship on the climate of the program. She meets with Marta and Kerene to address their issues transparently. She lets them know that she is stuck and they agree that they too are stuck. She asks them how they would feel if she reached out to a coach who specifically works with team dynamics. They are relieved and happy that Khadija has recognized the problem and brought them in to reflect on a solution, and are excited to start the work of repairing their communications. The coach is Roland, a man they all know from their church, who is kind and thoughtful. They feel safe enough to reflect honestly with him about what they perceive as the issues. Roland is a good listener and is able to activate curiosity with the team. He sees that a few miscommunications have led the team to this uncomfortable place and wonders with them about what needs to change and how that might happen. They each take time to think about how to ensure they are being understood by the others and not misinterpreted. In the end, the team commits to weekly check-ins, and if misunderstandings arise, they commit to finding ways of letting each other know they are being challenged.

Let's explore three levels of the commitment *refine communication: you and your identity, you with another,* and *you in a group.*

Refine Communication: You and Your Identity

The ways we speak, listen, and understand messages are uniquely our own. Our attitudes and beliefs about communication begin at birth as our caregivers interact with us, and later, as we have varied experiences with other people, our styles evolve over time.

❖ How has your identity shaped your style of communicating (your family of origin, your place of birth, your culture, race, gender, taboos, expectations, manners)?

_____

_____

_____

_____

❖ In what ways, if any, have you changed as a communicator over time? What were the influences that led to the changes?

_____

_____

_____

_____

❖ What are some lessons you have learned about effective communication? How have you applied them (in face-to-face conversations, in written communication, on social media, etc.)?

_____

_____

_____

_____

❖ When you think about yourself as a communicator, what do you notice about your tone, facial expressions, body language, word choices, pace and volume of speech?

_____

_____

_____

_____

❖ When you think about refining communication, what's really important to you?

_____

_____

_____

_____

For Bella, *refine communication: me and my identity* means learning to trust her own voice and advocate for herself. Bella tells her story:

> After I had my baby, I made the decision to go back to work at the childcare center where I could bring him. I knew it was best for my baby to breastfeed him. When I tried to speak with my mom and aunts about going back to work and breastfeeding my son, their southern upbringing (and mine), their lack of support and encouragement, and their intense criticism caused me to shut down. I lost my voice, I doubted my abilities, and I questioned every decision. My co-teacher Lakshmi, a twenty-year veteran at the program, and many years my senior with grown children of her own, began talking with me about my frustrations. With Lakshmi, I could easily talk about what I knew to be best for my son, but with my mom, I just couldn't find the words, the right tone, or even the trust in my message. My identity as a daughter and niece were stronger than my identity as a mom, but I wanted to be a mom first and an advocate for my child. My mom and aunts thought it was a disgrace to discuss breastfeeding, let alone do it at work. Lakshmi encouraged me day by day by noticing what I was doing that was working. Her support helped me establish my identity as a mom. While my identity is my own, the messages I heard from Lakshmi allowed me to see myself in a way that I hadn't before. Lakshmi helped me find my voice and new ways to communicate with others as an advocate for what I think is right.

Refine Communication: You with Another

Communication with another is about resonance and dissonance — whether you and the other person understand each other's meaning. As an Optimistic Leader, you can only change yourself and hope that it has an impact on the other person. With the commitment to *refine communication*, when it's challenging, ask yourself, "Is there something I can do to find the right fit?"

❖ Think about assumptions you may have around communication. Are there certain people you're more comfortable communicating with than others? Why do you think so?

_____

_____

_____

_____

❖ When you're communicating with another person, what are some ways you try to make the conversation two-way?

_____

_____

_____

_____

❖ Whether you are writing an email, speaking directly with the person, sending a text, or talking on the phone, how do you begin the communication? How do you tailor it to different people depending on the nature of your relationship?

_____

_____

_____

_____

❖ What are some ways you assess whether you are communicating effectively with another?

_____

_____

_____

_____

_____

❖ How do you ask for clarification if you find it difficult to understand another person?

_____

_____

_____

_____

_____

For Bella, *refine communication: you with another* means noticing how she communicates and how it changes with different people.

I notice that I have different ways of communicating with men and women and I'm not sure if that's because of how I was raised. I'm more reserved when communicating with men because I don't want to come across as flirtatious. When a person is new to me, I don't want to assume that person is receiving my message or that I'm receiving hers. One story comes to mind about my tendency to make assumptions about another person's style of communicating. When I was an assistant director at a childcare center, there was a master teacher, Sue, who was fifteen years older than me. It was a strange dynamic because though I was her supervisor, Sue was much more experienced. I'm outgoing and you can sort of read me like a book. Sue was more reserved and I made assumptions that she knew everything about teaching and really didn't want me around. Her classroom was effective. I thought to myself, "She's fine and she's ignoring me so I'll leave her alone." After a while I realized that I had to find a way to communicate with her and that perhaps I could invite a conversation by suggesting she might want to do some workshops for our upcoming local conference. She was shocked and sort of delighted. She responded by saying, "I'd be really nervous about doing that. Do you think I have something to offer other teachers?" This conversation changed our relationship. She decided to submit a proposal for a workshop at a conference and knowing that I had done many workshops before, she asked for my help.

Refine Communication: You in a Group

Have you noticed that in a meeting, one group member can influence the way others communicate? Sometimes one person dominates the conversation, leaving little or no space for others to participate. Or one or two group members might be annoyed and remain silent but their body language and facial expressions speak loudly and affect the mood of others, restricting or preventing interactions. Think about how you practice *refine communication* in a group.

❖ What are some ways you check to see if the messages you convey in a group are heard and understood?

_____

_____

_____

_____

_____

_____

❖ Think about how you convey messages in group settings. Do you take time to think, write your ideas down first, listen to see how others respond, or do your thinking while speaking?

_____

_____

_____

_____

_____

_____

❖ How do you wish others would communicate in group settings?

_____

_____

_____

_____

_____

❖ How do you use nonverbal communication in a group setting?

_____

_____

_____

_____

_____

As Bella practices *refine communication: you in a group*, she describes an experience in her role as coach in which she is challenging herself to be brave and influence the group's willingness to be open with each other.

> *I facilitate a remote coaching group with six others. Our purpose is to discuss successes and challenges we're having as coaches and problem-solve together. A group expectation is that when we use Zoom, the video will be on and we'll mute voices when there's background noise. During this particular discussion, Chrystal shares that she gets annoyed when one of her coaches is driving during their Zoom coaching sessions. I wanted to explode because Chrystal does this when we have our one-on-ones, and she always has an excuse for why. It took all my self-control not to say, "Excuse me? You do that all the time." Instead, I thought about how I could communicate in a way that would strengthen the group and make our communication more open and honest. I shifted from annoyance to curiosity and decided to extend her grace. I said, "One director I coach also drives when we have our Zoom sessions. I'm wondering why." Chrystal was the first to respond, asking, "Does it annoy you?" "Well yes," I said, "it does, but what I if I give her some grace and think about all she has to do during the day?" Rhea chimed in, " I never thought about that. I guess it is hard to find time for all these Zoom calls and still be fully present for the health and safety needs of the children in our programs." After the coaching session was over, I got a text from Chrystal. She wrote, "Can we chat?" I gave her a call and the first thing she said was, "Thanks for not calling me out in the meeting. I know I'm guilty of driving when we have our one-on-ones and it didn't even dawn on me when I started complaining that I do it too."*

Bella's stories of *you and your identity, you with another,* and *you in a group* illustrate how each commitment requires deep reflection, and that we continue to grow and change as we have more experiences. When we show others that we want to build a relationship, that we are trustworthy, and that we're willing to be vulnerable, it goes a long way in our efforts to support adult learners and model how adults can be with children.

Thinking About Your Practice

1. Think about what it would be like if you and those around you thought more about the commitment to *refine communication.* How might the emotional climate of your workplace improve?

_____

_____

_____

_____

_____

2. Here are some questions to think about:

❖ Why is it important to you to refine communication in your work with colleagues, children, and families?

_____

_____

_____

_____

_____

❖ In what ways are you already effective in communicating your ideas, thoughts, and needs?

_____

_____

_____

_____

_____

❖ How can you practice remaining aware of your verbal, nonverbal, and written communication techniques in situations that are easy or challenging?

_____

_____

_____

_____

_____

_____

❖ How do you practice active listening for understanding and to inform your own ability to communicate effectively?

_____

_____

_____

_____

_____

_____

❖ What are some questions you would feel comfortable asking to help ensure mutual clarity and understanding?

_____

_____

_____

_____

_____

3. Begin to collect examples of how you're practicing the commitment _refine communication_ to _nurture relationships_ at all three levels.

_____

_____

_____

_____

_____

"I am neither clever nor especially gifted. I am only very, very curious"

– Albert Einstein

Activate Curiosity

Nichole recalls: *I was once in a business meeting with about ten others to make some very big decisions that would impact a significant number of people. A detailed notetaker, I was writing down everything people were saying. As the conversation continued, I realized that the word "they" was consistently used. "They" just need and "they" don't and "they" should.*

I was beginning to take offense on behalf of "they." Looking at my notes as a strategy to calm myself, I noticed that the word "they" had been used seven times in twenty minutes. This made me very uncomfortable, yet I wasn't sure if I should say anything.

It seemed disrespectful to talk about a group of people as they, as if they had no identity and no value. As if they weren't worth the effort of getting to know them or the time to try to understand their world. I remembered how it feels to be a part of "they." As a woman of color, it was a term I was all too familiar with. When the word "they" is used in this way, it automatically creates a divide between you and them. It is the opposite of connecting, collaborating, and forging teams. Our words send messages. When we say "they" we are giving ourselves and others the message that somehow the other person(s) is less than. More a thing than a person. We must refine our communication so that our words send the message we want people to hear.

And while it is possible that no disrespect was meant by "they," I simply couldn't sit in that space without calling attention to it.

So, I sat up and asked, "Excuse me, but who is 'they'? I want us to really think about the words we are using. They are a part of us, the system that supports and educates children. We have to use language that reflects that. Language that reminds us that we are connected and in this together." I would love to say that from that day forward, I never heard the word "they" in reference to another group of people, but I do. And I am still asking the question, "Who is 'they'?"

Activate curiosity to find connections and continue learning means exploring, investigating, questioning, researching, and wondering. We are all born learners, naturally curious to understand the world around us, listening to sounds, looking around at everything in sight, and grabbing whatever is in our reach. We begin exploring with curiosity even more as we crawl, then walk, begin to eat, and experiment with language. Gradually, this natural curiosity is influenced by those who care for and educate us. We are the adults in the child's ecosystem who help them cultivate curiosity.

Consider the possibilities for children if everyone around them turned worry into wonder. When you *activate curiosity*, you are more willing to take risks, experiment, and try things out. A curious and open mind invites learning. When you're willing to ask questions, consider possibilities, and persist in tackling obstacles, there are so many more opportunities for growth and change.

Rather than worrying about failure, the curious leader knows that errors can promote learning. When working with children and families, curiosity means letting go of your agenda and watching and listening in order to learn what matters to the child or his family. This may require a degree of holding back and watching or listening before saying or doing anything. As Optimistic Leaders, it is imperative for us to continue to *activate curiosity* so that we keep learning and serve as models for children.

Here's a scenario with and without *activating curiosity*. In the first, Regina jumps to a conclusion without wondering why her colleague is behaving out of character.

Regina, a center director, noticed some behavior changes in Sally, one of her most talented teachers. Sally had started responding to questions with one-word answers, and no longer smiled and chatted with Regina as she used to. A few days later, Sally started leaving the building for lunch every day rather than joining the other teachers in the lounge. Regina felt certain that Sally's sudden withdrawal from her and the staff meant she was actively looking for another job.

As Regina continued to write her version of what was happening in her mind, she began to get angry. "I thought we were friends. I thought I could

"Curiosity is at the heart of lifelong learning. It not only gives children an advantage in school, but today's business leaders agree that it is also at the heart of thriving organizations."
—MARILYN PRICE-MITCHELL, 2015

trust her. If she's looking for another job, why wouldn't she tell me? How can I replace her? She's one of the best teachers I have."

Regina finally reached a crescendo of anger when she received a leave request from Sally a few days later. She just knew this meant Sally was taking time off to go to a job interview at another center. Regina angrily grabbed the request and marched to Sally's room. "You know Sally, if you're planning on leaving, you can tell me."

"What are you talking about?" asked Sally, clearly confused and insulted by Regina's accusatory tone.

"Well, you aren't really talking to anyone, you've started leaving the building during lunch, and now you've requested a day off. What am I supposed to think?"

Sally sighs. "I'm requesting leave because I've finally saved enough money to go to the dentist. I've had a toothache for several weeks. I've been going home on my lunch break to take medicine and put an ice pack on my face."

"Oh," says Regina, realizing that she'd made assumptions and now had to do relationship repair.

In this scenario, Regina stops to *activate curiosity* about the changes in Sally's behavior, with a completely different outcome.

Regina, a center director, noticed some behavior changes in Sally, one of her most talented teachers. Sally had started responding to questions with one-word answers, and no longer smiled and chatted with Regina as she used to. A few days later, Sally started leaving the building for lunch every day rather than joining the other teachers in the lounge as usual. Regina notices the changes in Sally's behavior and wonders if she's okay. She reminds herself of what it was like to be a classroom teacher and makes a note to observe and offer Sally more support over the next few days.

She begins to think of all the reasons Sally's behavior is changing. Maybe she's looking for another job. Then she pauses and decides to activate her curiosity. Sally and I have a good working relationship. Rather than guess and write my own narrative, I'll talk with her.

Regina goes to Sally's room, greeting her and quietly observing as normal. She notices Sally isn't talking as much with the children and instead is doing more of the observational notes while the assistant teachers facilitate small groups. That makes her curious, as Sally is a masterful teacher who is known for how she stays fully present to engage children in conversations. When the children went outside with the assistant teachers, Regina asked Sally if she'd be willing to take a walk with her. "Sure," said Sally.

Regina says, "Sally, you are such a wonderful teacher and colleague. You are always intentional in connecting with people to engage them in thoughtful conversations. Everyone feels seen and smart when you're around. I notice that you've not been talking as much lately. I don't want to pry, but I wanted to take time to connect with you to see if you wanted to talk or if I could be of help to you in some way."

Sally's eyes begin to well up. "Thank you. I've had a toothache for several weeks. I've been saving my money to go to the dentist. I've been taking over-the-counter pain medication in the mornings, but it wears off by noon. During my lunch break, I've been going to my car to take more medication and to put an ice pack on my jaw. I requested time off because I now have enough to pay for the dentist visit. "

Regina responds, "Sally, I am so sorry you've been in pain. You don't have to talk anymore. Would it be okay if I think about ways I can support you while you're recovering from the procedure?"

By stopping and activating curiosity, Regina was able to suspend judgment and show up as a supportive colleague, and strengthened the relationship rather than having to do relationship repair.

Let's explore the three levels of the commitment *activate curiosity: you and your identity, you with another,* and *you in a group.*

Activate Curiosity: You and Your Identity

The first place to think about curiosity is to be curious about yourself. Take some time to think about what you learned about curiosity as a child and how this may have evolved over time based on people you know and experiences you've had. Think about *activate curiosity: you and your identity* as an opportunity to reflect on your thoughts and feelings and the influences that have shaped who you are as a curious person.

❖ In what ways has your identity shaped you as a curious person (early experiences, gender, race)?

My parents
Having male siblings

❖ Who and what have influenced who you have become as a curious person?

My mentors. Supervisors My mom.
CFE "What is the intention?"

❖ What sparks your curiosity?

Everything.
People's behaviors.
→ Especially in college.

❖ How do you approach learning about new ideas, concepts, and experiences?

Reading about it.
Putting it into practice

❖ Are there people or experiences you've had that have influenced you as a curious person?

_____

_____

_____

_____

To illustrate you and your identity for the commitment to *activate curiosity*, here's a story about Aram, an early learning educator, now in his fifties, who began as a teacher, became a coach, then an associate program director, and finally a director. He describes his understanding of curiosity.

When I was growing up, I had an older brother who was really smart. He seemed to always have the answers to every question. I learned early on that being curious was simply about finding the answer, and I was tenacious in doing it, but once I got the answer, I was done. For example, if there was a history question at school, I wanted to find the answer, and when I did, it never occurred to me to keep digging. I actually got anxious when I had trouble finding an answer. I don't recall being encouraged to go on journeys of learning. My early memory of play was not about exploration. Rather, it was reenactments. My big brother would initiate games like "cops and robbers" and the script was mostly written by him. My really big shift as a curious person—having a strong feeling of interest to know—came when I began teaching young children. I was absolutely delighted watching their curiosity and it sparked my own. The children taught me how to be curious and how to be playful!

Activate Curiosity: You with Another

You with another is always about relationships — one on one with children and with adults. As an Optimistic Leader, think about how you use curiosity in relationships to get to know individuals, to deepen trust and nurture the relationship.

Next, think about whether you choose to be with people who ignite your curiosity because you share a spirit of wanting to know more, or because that person helps ignite your curiosity. Or perhaps, you might be a catalyst for another person's curiosity.

❖ Think about how you enter interactions with children. Reflect on whether you are curious to understand what they are thinking and feeling or do you tend to make assumptions?

_____

_____

_____

_____

_____

❖ Reflect on these same questions about adults.

_____

_____

_____

_____

_____

❖ How do you use curiosity to quiet assumptions and judgments about another person?

_____

_____

_____

_____

_____

❖ When you meet someone for the first time, what questions do you ask?

_____

_____

_____

_____

_____

❖ Think about others you are drawn to because they bring out your curious nature. What is it they do that nurtures your curiosity?

_____

_____

_____

_____

_____

❖ When you disagree with someone, can you stay open to learn more about their point of view?

_____

_____

_____

_____

_____

To illustrate you with another for the commitment *activate curiosity*, Aram describes how curiosity created a very positive interaction he had as the associate director of an early learning program. He met with the family to talk about the program's observations of their fourteen-month-old baby.

> *Aram wants to make sure he demonstrates his intentions to learn through his interactions. He explains: We have a strong team of teachers, all with special education degrees. Mathias, fourteen months, was in our baby room and his giggle delighted us all. His smile was contagious. With an adult close by, he explored toys and looked at books, but when an unfamiliar person came into the room, Mathias cried. Transitions set Mathias off with a tantrum. We experimented with many strategies and relied on our program's specialists to support Mathias's success. We talked regularly with Mathias's parents, listening to their observations at home, sharing our appreciation and delight as well as our concerns. We maintained a supportive and curious stance, conveying at every turn that Mathias's success was our primary goal. When it was time to introduce*

the idea of an evaluation to the parents so that we could learn more, I began by inviting them to share recent observations of Mathias at home. Mathias's mom began to cry. I followed with some of the same observations at school and the many strategies we continue to try. I was very careful to frame the need for an evaluation as another step on our path of curiosity—to learn more about how to support Mathias's success. It wasn't an easy conversation and yet we all agreed by the end that an evaluation was the best way to get another pair of well-trained eyes to help us support Mathias. I'm sure that our willingness to maintain a stance of curiosity was key to the conversation going well.

Activate Curiosity: You in a Group

Groups can get into ruts pretty easily. Behaviors become predictable, such as which person talks, who makes jokes, what topics are easy to address, and where people get stuck. This is true with groups of children and adults and it can also be true with family groups. As an Optimistic Leader in a group, think about how you support groups in finding meaningful connections, deepening relationships, and learning more.

❖ How do you use curiosity to show up in a group?

_____

_____

_____

_____

_____

_____

❖ How do you use curiosity to quiet assumptions when you're in a group?

_____

_____

_____

_____

_____

_____

❖ In what ways do you use questions to help a group stay open and curious about a topic?

_____
_____
_____
_____
_____
_____
_____

❖ What happens in a group to shut down your curiosity?

_____
_____
_____
_____
_____
_____
_____

To illustrate you in a group for the commitment *activate curiosity*, Aram, now the director of an early learning program, shares a story about how his faculty was upset about professional development and his struggle to maintain the commitment of curiosity.

*As Aram continues his practice of **activate curiosity: you in a group**, he focuses on himself in a group. Aram explains: My assistant director, Megan, and I were curious to hear the teachers' suggestions for professional development in the coming year. We used focus groups and surveys to gather data about topics and delivery methods. We implemented the first workshop about a topic that everyone had chosen, and used the techniques the teachers requested: small-group work, classroom visits, and time to practice and apply new ideas. During our debrief afterward, Megan and I agreed that despite seeking input from everyone, the day was flat. End-of-day reflection forms showed teachers' dissatisfaction. Quieting our resentment and holding on to curiosity, we sent a* *note to teachers inviting them to a conversation about what might have gone awry. Four people agreed to meet and we began with an open-ended prompt. "Thinking about the PD day we just had, what activated your curiosity?" Each person described something they found interesting—a conversation, a new idea, or a classroom visit. Next, we focused on what went wrong. One teacher candidly observed that the staff is in a rut. "Everyone comes to PD and sits with friends. A negative attitude prevails and it's as if nobody wants to enjoy the experience. Some of us want to like it but are afraid to go against the crowd." This was an amazing aha for both Megan and me. This group agreed to meet regularly to see how we could shift the dynamic among the staff to create more vibrant and engaging professional learning opportunities. One of the first things we implemented was assigning groups and structuring the activities so that everyone worked with new people. The energy changed quickly so we knew we were on the path to more productive professional learning. It took discipline for Megan and me to quiet our annoyance and to maintain curiosity to keep moving beyond our frustration. By the end of the year, the PD reflections were more detailed, and people took time to describe what they valued and offered rich suggestions for future events.*

The stories Aram offered describe his path with curiosity and how as his roles shifted, so did his thinking about curiosity.

When we activate curiosity, we can more easily quiet our assumptions and implicit biases and stay open to learning. As Optimistic Leaders, we invite you to practice the commitment of activate curiosity so that children can learn and grow in safe, comfortable environments and have adults around them who model intentionality.

Thinking About Your Practice

1. Think about what it would be like if you and those around you thought more about the commitment to *activate curiosity.* How might the emotional climate of your workplace improve?

_____

_____

_____

_____

_____

_____

_____

_____

2. Here are some questions to think about:

❖ Why is it important for you to remain curious about your work in support of children and families?

_____

_____

_____

_____

_____

_____

❖ What are you good at and how can you build upon it further?

_____

_____

_____

_____

_____

_____

_____

❖ How do you activate curiosity in yourself (read an article, have a conversation, observe other people)?

_____

_____

_____

_____

_____

_____

_____

❖ What is the importance of wondering and asking yourself questions about the unknown as they arise?

_____

_____

_____

_____

_____

_____

_____

_____

3. Begin to collect examples of you practicing the commitment _activate curiosity_ at all three levels.

_____

_____

_____

_____

_____

_____

_____

_____

_____

Moving Ahead

Making the Five Commitments of Optimistic Leader Your Own

Practicing the Five Commitments of Optimistic Leadership is not about mastery. Rather, it is an ongoing reflective endeavor that we believe can support all of us in making our lives better. We find that our relationships with colleagues, our families, and our friends are healthier and more gratifying. Each of us approaches the practice a little differently. Sometimes it is simply a pause before speaking or taking an action. Other times, it's starting the day with a five-minute reflection. We also find that while the practice is our own, using it in conversations with groups deepens our understanding, strengthens our relationships, and is really enjoyable. We encourage you to experiment with practicing the five commitments in a way that is right for you.

Larramie shares: *I express to the children daily the importance of being themselves, being open, comfortable with yourself. I use the five commitments to guide me and my actions. The real question for me is how committed are we? How much are we willing to put into this work? How far are we willing to go? How much energy do we have? I'm hoping that we really follow through, not just at work or with the children in our homes. Are we thinking impact at the grocery store, at the gas station, driving down the street. Are we cultivating self-awareness as we go through our everyday lives? Are we being the best version of ourselves, not only for those close to us but with the people that we meet in our day-to day-lives? I'm challenging myself every day to try to be fully committed to who I say I am, what I'm doing. And I think we all have to challenge ourselves to be the best version of ourselves and be fully committed to the five commitments in every single way.*

Kenecha shares: *The Five Commitments of Optimistic Leaders have given me a true outline for purpose on my path to help make a positive difference for the children and families in communities across Mississippi. Using the commitments allows me to think more deeply about my impact, engage in open and honest dialogue regarding change, create goals beyond the now, and use self-reflection in meaningful ways.*

Marneshia shares: *For me, being aware of how I show up in a situation has definitely changed. I'm more cognizant of my presence, my expressions, and my reactions. Applying the commitments of Optimistic Leaders, not just at the preschool, but just in every area of my life. I use them in my adult-to-adult interactions, with my co-workers, family, and friends, and definitely with how I relate to our students. I recognize that they are little people who have their own opinions and feelings. I remind myself and my staff that we're not raising children, we're raising adults. Even though they're small, they have thoughts and opinions and feelings and we need to engage them the same way we would engage each other.*

About Leading for Children

The three big questions that inform our work at Leading for Children are:

- How can we change early learning so that what happens by, for, and with adults is equitable and antiracist, so that we are true role models for children?

- How can we support every adult in children's lives to be the leaders children deserve?

- How can we promote a culture of optimism so that children grow up hopeful around adults who solve problems together and see a path forward?

At Leading for Children, we have chosen to support children's learning through transformative relationships. We believe that because systems are comprised of people, transformative relationships must drive systems change. As we said earlier, systems get stronger when the people within them at every level are deeply motivated to think and work in new ways on behalf of a larger vision of quality and exemplary practices for children and families.

Our conviction is that the system has to be changed by the people within it rather than the people outside. "Systemic change" is often code for: "Let's go into a community with a top-down solution and fix people by telling them what they need, or by defining an operating system that is not authored by people working inside it or affected by it." People living within an oppressive system know what they need and what must change. In our Learning Networks, every member works together as Optimistic Leaders for children, becoming agents of change who can change their own programs and the broader community.

Together we can transform early learning. Please join us.

Acknowledgements

The ideas encompassed within this journal emerged from years of learning with and from educators and family members across the country and to them we are so grateful for the knowledge and lived experience they bring to children's lives each day.

To our colleagues on the Leading for Children National Optimistic Leaders Advisory Council, we deeply appreciate your willingness to think with us about equity and leadership, to share your personal and professional stories, insights, and challenges about how to "show up" as Optimistic Leaders for children. Gratitude to Serene Stevens, Jill Gunderman, Tara Skiles, Sharmaine Thomas-Binns, Tia Walters, Tunga Otis, Irene Garneau, Maria Rosado, Silvia Salcido, Casey Sims, Larramie Sylvester, Robin Hancock, and Margo Dichtelmiller.

During the past three years, our understanding of Optimistic Leadership has been stretched through our partnership with April May and Kenecha Brooks-Smith and Mississippi Leadership for Children. To each Learning Network member, together we expanded our collective understanding of the importance of modeling Optimistic Leadership for Children. Thank you to the educators, staff and family members at West Point Christian Preschool, Global Connection Learning Center, Early Encounters Preschool and Learning Center, Excel by Five, and Mississippi Community Colleague Board Early Childhood Academy. We are grateful for what you do every day to ensure that Mississippi's children will have every opportunity for success, now and in the future: Akacia McGee, Alexas Rayford-Page, Amber Robinson, Angela McCaskill, Anna Drummond, Ashley Mitchell Armstrong, Bernita Porter, Bettye Shepherd, Brittany Longino, Brittany Lenoir, Cambre McCullum, Camelody Miller, Carl Henderson, Charity Brown, Charnessa Alexander, Cheryl Stewart, Cortnie Dorsey, Deborah Gilbert, Eddena (Mona) Lockhart, Eileen Beazley, Erica Dixon, Essie Goode, Evelyn Nelson, Gina Kodger, Herman Sylvester, Hollie Ridgeway, Jacqueline Hibbler, Jasmine Andrews, Jasmine Dedrick, Jeardine Robinson, Jennifer Funchness, Jevelyn Smith-Young, Kara McCaskill, Khiana Esco, Kimberly Hall, La Shonda Murphy, LaMya LeFlore, Larramie Sylvester, Latasha Betts, LaToya McKellar, LaVern Newton, Linda Brewer, Lisa Bonds, Marion Douglas, Markeisha Rhodes, Marneshia Cathey, Meagan Tate, Melia Turner-Morris, Mimi Rosca, Monica Price, Monique Thomas, Nancy Sylvester, Patti Fleming, Precious Morgan, Qymika Williams, Reggie Taylor,

Robin Griffith, Rosie (Tina) Davis, Samwondra Conner, Shuronda Claiborne-Common, Stephanie Lucas, Suellen Santymer-Clark, Tamika Leflore, Tammy McCullum, Tanakia Richardson, Tara McGee, Temica Fowler, Tessa LeAnn Ridenour, Theresa Tate-Briggs, Tia Walters, Tina McDonald, Tomekee Thomas, Tunga Otis, and Yamasheta Powe.

To our partners in New York City — Mimi Basso, Loren DeNicola, and the faculty at West Side Montessori School and to Amy Warden and Elena Jaime at The Brick Church School, thank you for practicing the Five Commitments of Optimistic Leader and sharing your experiences along the way. We have been fortunate to learn with and from many educators across the state of Wyoming. We would like to offer a special thanks to Nikki Baldwin, Tyler Gonzalez, Kara Cossel, Liz Goddard, Jennifer Zook, Stephanie Rino, Char Norris, Lauren Carlisle, and Ellie Gardner for your persistent curiosity and wisdom regarding the commitments and what it takes internally to consistently practice them.

Special thanks to Diana Courson, Hope Lesane, Gary Romano, Alison LaRocca, and Khaatim Sherrer El who offered guidance at every turn as we developed the manuscript. Thanks to Joelle Gruber Wheatley and Chris Maxwell for their research along the way. Members of the LFC team, Christine Shrader and Lauren Farmer, thank you for your willingness to always be thought partners.

Thank you, Lisa Holton for your vision and guidance as we shaped the national Optimistic Leadership campaign that was vital to the development of the book and for your steward-ship throughout the production process. Gretchen Henderson, you're amazing and we could never have done this without your generous and gracious direction. Ahmed Yearwood, your ability to listen to us and our partners across the country and transform what you hear in so many different ways is unique and we love that we get to work with you. To our designer, Angela Corbo Gier, you make magic on the page and we are grateful to you for making this book beautiful. Finally, we are indebted to Hope Matthhiessen and Jane Cavolina for their editorial expertise and guidance.

References

Barsade, S., & O'Neill, O. (2020, December 16). *Manage Your Emotional Culture*. Harvard Business Review. https://hbr.org/2016/01/manage-your-emotional-culture

Children's Defense Fund. (2018, May 17). *It's Hard to be What You Can't See — Children's Defense Fund.* https://www.childrensdefense.org/child-watch-columns/health/2015/its-hard-to-be-what-you-cant-see/

Hewitt, M. B. (2005). *The Importance of Taking a Strength-Based Perspective.* Crisis Prevention Institue. https://www.crisisprevention.com/Blog/The-Importance-of-Taking-a-Strength-Based-Perspect

Oertwig, S. & Holland, A. (2014). Improving Instruction. In S. Ritchie & L. Guttman (Eds.) *FirstSchool: Transforming PreK-3rd grade for African American, Latino, and low-income children* (pp. 102-124). New York: Teachers College Press.

Price-Mitchell, M. (2015, April 15). *Curiosity: The Heart of Lifelong Learning. Psychology Today.* https://www.psychologytoday.com/us/blog/the-moment-youth/201504/curiosity-the-heart-lifelong-learning

Shidler, L. (2010). Teacher-to-Teacher: The Heart of the Coaching Model. *Young Children, 65*(4), 70–75. https://eric.ed.gov/?id=EJ898725

Sinek, S. (2020, April 6). *Optimism vs. Positivity.* YouTube. https://www.youtube.com/watch?v=roDLXM70du0

About the Authors

Judy Jablon is founder and executive director of Leading for Children. She is the author of numerous publications and videos, including *Powerful Interactions: How to Connect with Children to Extend their Learning*.

Nichole Parks is Director of Programs at Leading for Children. During her career, she has served in diverse roles in early learning including Quality Rating Improvement System Program Coordinator with Arkansas State University Childhood Services.

Laura Ensler is an Advisor on Strategic Partnerships for Leading for Children. She is the Founder of FirstStepNYC and the NYC Early Childhood Leadership Initiative.

CPSIA information can be obtained
at www.ICGtesting.com
Printed in the USA
LVHW071455230421
685335LV00013B/54

* 9 7 8 0 5 7 8 8 3 4 3 6 8 *